ALICE
-N-
CRACK LAND

To
LaMarr
Be blessed

To Mort Bessel
[signature, illegible]

ALICE -N- CRACK LAND

La Wanda
Marrero

TATE PUBLISHING & Enterprises

Published by Tate Publishing & Enterprises, LLC
127 E. Trade Center Terrace | Mustang, Oklahoma 73064 USA
1.888.361.9473 | www.tatepublishing.com

Tate Publishing is committed to excellence in the publishing industry. The company reflects the philosophy established by the founders, based on Psalm 68:11,
"The Lord gave the word and great was the company of those who published it."

Published in the United States of America

ISBN: 978-1-60604-146-8
1. Family & Relationships: Abuse
2. Inspiration: Motivational: Biography & Autobiography
09.06.02

ACKNOWLEDGEMENTS

To Elder Pete, my brother in Christ, a wounded heart is an open target; thanks for holding your peace.

To my Shiloh Family, thanks for your love, support and carrying the weight of my purpose with me.

To my daughters, the best sample is to live by example.

To my son, to whom much is given, much is required. Walk in the light.

To my ghostwriter, Julie Whitten, thank you for pulling, pushing, and prying. You made a difference in my life as a child and now as I've grown into a woman. Let's keep laughing.

To Marie, thanks for all your years of wisdom, love, and support.

To my mothers, may this be the proudest day for you in my life.

To my Auntie Cedra, the Dingahs, and women everywhere—let's forgive, forget, move past, and live life in its fullness.

To my friends and co-workers, thanks for your ongoing words of encouragement.

To Jerry Herman, thanks for the challenge and the red marks on my papers.

To my Pastor George Lee, with tears of joy, I say thank you for speaking life into me, and your no-pity-party policy for me.

To the Simmons family, walk in God's victory.

To my ex-husband, thank you for what was real. I've learned my true value.

To Abby, my best friend, thank you for telling me to stop talking about writing and start doing some writing. Rest in peace, I love and will see you soon.

To my uncle Ted Jr., may the Lord's peace and mercy find you on the road to Damascus and his grace lift you.

To all the people who had the courage to share their testimony, thank you, for without you no one would know Alice.

To Pastor James Long and the True Faith Baptist Church for their help with the bruises on my heart.

To my ancestors, the secrets have no more power. May peace prevail in our family.

TABLE OF CONTENTS

FOREWORD

Alice N Crackland is a forthright, enthralling, provocative journey through darkness into the light. The author's relentless search for the truth and her willingness to accept what she finds is captivating. She faces life on life's terms, always willing to see the blessings and the humor in her struggles. She has an amazing ability to rise above the devastating confusion of being abused by those who were supposed to love and protect her. Readers from all walks of life and personal persuasions will be inspired by the resiliency of the human spirit and filled with compassion for the author.

The reader gets to witness the squalid street life of pimps, prostitutes, drug users, and dealers that the author lived in and by the grace of God was not consumed by. The author describes eloquently the intense conflict of being both an addict and a mother. She wanders through the maze of *Crackland* and guided by her benevolent pastor and congregation, she awakens in the "Wonderland of Love." This book was not only healing for the author and many family members, it had the miraculous effect of uniting them with renewed understanding, compassion, and respect for each other. It has the potential to do the same for the reader.

Marie Simmons
Author of *My Life—It's Nothing Personal, and Neither is Yours*

9

GRAY AREAS

I remember the night my grandmother was raped. She came home with her clothes torn, and she was very upset. Everybody was up in a roar, and people were excited and kept asking her questions. *What happened? What happened? Who? What?* Grannie Gran just kept shaking her head. She is a quiet woman, very secretive, but she must have told them what happened to her. They decided they were going to take her to the hospital, and they left Kent, my uncle, in charge of the six kids. I was four, and I remember feeling scared when I heard he was going to take care of us. He had been in the service, and when he came home, he was addicted to heroin. He would shoot up in the bathroom, and everybody knew he was on drugs. Nobody talked about it, though. He was instructed to feed us, and he made us pork and beans and hot dogs. Then he put us to bed.

I was in the downstairs bedroom, and I remember him picking me up and taking me up a long stairway to the upstairs bathroom. Kent was a short, muscular, dark-skinned black man with thick square-framed glasses. His smile was crooked, and he always smelled of sweat. I was afraid, but I was too scared to cry. It had a familiar feeling, but there was no conversation between us. I knew what he wanted me to do. I had done it so many times before, with him. He set me on the toilet seat lid, and I looked at the cracks and the mildew stains on the walls. In the grain of the doorframe, someone had carved a smiling face, and we called it Peeping Tom.

He unzipped his pants, and I closed my eyes. He had a bitter taste. He made grunting sounds. He never said anything, and he never tried to penetrate me. After he finished, I think I took myself back downstairs and got in bed. I never told anyone. By this time, I thought it was normal. I thought nobody cared.

Later as an adult, I talked to his sister, my aunt, Auntie Cedra. I was at her house one day, and out of the blue, she said, "I know what happened to you. He used to do the same thing to me. He would leave a nickel up on my dresser." She knew I was having problems with men because of it, and it was her way of comforting me. I was shocked because I didn't think anybody knew. She said, "I tried to tell them about you, but they wouldn't listen to me, so I knew they wouldn't believe that it was happening to me."

My earliest memory of my abuse is was of Kent and me sitting in the front seat of an old broken down car parked next to the apple tree in the back yard. It was Uncle Harry's old blue station wagon. I remember him telling me to be quiet. He was sitting in the driver's seat, looking around. Then exposing himself, he pushed my head down. He threatened me and told me not to tell anybody. Another memory is of a cemented cubbyhole off to the right at the foot of the stairs in the back yard. I remember feeling all clammy, the dampness, and I felt smothered and suffocated in the tiny hole, as he continued to do what he had done so many times before. I hated what he was doing to me, and I was gripped by terror.

I recall vividly the last morning that I lived in St. Louis. Grannie got up very early that morning and had her old silver percolator on making a strong brew of coffee. She had prepared a feast for me to eat: toast, eggs, bacon, sausage, and my favorite—Cream of Wheat. I remember this as such a happy moment between us. A month before, the family had been sitting around the living room, and Grandma Mattie (Marie's mother), and Marie were visiting. Marie suddenly asked, "Who wants to go to California?"

I lifted my hand and gave a great big shout—"*I do!*" Apparently my great-auntie Marie, Grannie's sister, wanted to help raise some children in the family, so my "*I do*" got me picked to be the one to go.

Grannie was crying in my Cream of Wheat that morning, and she didn't cry often. I had no idea what was the matter, perhaps it had to do with my leaving, or maybe she thought I had done something bad. She explained to me again that I was going to catch a train with my great-grandma Mattie to my new home in California with Marie.

I was a little scared, because I didn't know what to expect, but I knew I wanted something different. I had seen Marie when she came to visit. She was always kissing all the kids, those that she knew and those that she didn't. At the time, I didn't know how this would affect what was going on with me and Kent, but since he wasn't going, I felt eager to go. The train ride took about three days, and it was so freeing to be on that train! To break free from my old situation—to be going to something new! On the third day, I woke up and realized I was really leaving my past in St. Louis, or so I thought. To this day, I still love the sound of a train.

Marie was there to greet us at the Fresno train station. She was standing with her arms stretched wide open. I was so excited to be going *home* with her and she even had a bedroom, which was to be my very own! The house was so huge and there was a pool in the back yard! I was overwhelmed, but happy! She gave me so much attention, took me shopping, and bought me anything I wanted in the grocery store. For the first time I felt like I really mattered to somebody. I decided I never would tell her what happened in St. Louis, because I feared then she would not want anything to do with me and she would send me back. I felt like that was a dirty little secret, and that maybe I was sent away as punishment for the bad things I'd been doing. As I grew older, I wondered if anyone in St. Louis knew what Kent was doing to me and sent me away to protect me.

I had left 4014 Maffitt Street in St. Louis for two years and then had returned for a visit when I was twelve. Kent was still living with my grandmother in the same house. I was walking down the hallway. I looked into the bedroom, and he said, "Hey! Come here." I felt terrified again, but I still went in. This time I was different. I had been living with Marie and my Great Grandma Mattie in California, and had developed some personal power. I knew I was not going to allow it to happen again. He said, "Do you remember what we used to do?"

I said, "I don't know what you're talking about." There were no more sexual altercations with him.

A few years later, he moved to California to live in San Francisco, and we would often visit his house, but I never allowed myself to be alone with him. I noticed that he had three TV's on at the same time in one room, each with a different station. Sometimes he even had the radio on too. He was a very confused person. He never approached me sexually again, but feelings of fear and violation lingered on in me. The day he died was a day of rejoicing for me. I felt like that part of my past with him died. This was wishful thinking. I was empowered when Kent died, but it was false empowerment.

I had the same sense of power when Grannie Gran's brother, Baker Boy, died a few weeks ago. Years ago, I was living in Sausalito and Baker Boy was living there, too. He was tall and skinny, and always reeking of alcohol. His glasses were taped together and were always crooked on his face. He had a habit of pushing them up on one side. He was an excellent cook, but he never cleaned up the kitchen behind himself. He would use every pot and pan in the house. When I was around him, I had the same eerie feeling as when I was around Kent. I tried to keep myself out of sticky situations, trying never to be alone with him.

However, one day I went downstairs into the yellow bedroom, (my bedroom), and he was lying on the bed (my bed). I thought he was taking a nap, so trying not to wake him up, I crept into the bedroom looking for something. I looked at him, and he opened his eyes. He flung the covers off and revealed himself to me. It looked soft and wrinkled, and I remember smelling and tasting Kent again. I just looked at him and ran out of the bedroom, and I never told Marie or anyone else. *How could I tell her about something like that?* I think he was testing me to see if I would allow him to touch me... He had four or five daughters, and as an adult, I often wondered what he did to them. I spoke to them once, and they claimed that he never touched them because their mother sheltered them.

As a child, I can remember being moved around a lot. My mother's mental state was child-like and my father was unknown to me then. People circulated me between my grandfather, Ted Sr., and whatever girlfriend he was with that month, his mother Grandma Bonnie, and my grandmother, Grannie Gran. Grandpa Ted was a very handsome man. He had burgundy processed hair that was always slicked back, and a host of women, many of whom were hairdressers. He drove a red-and-white drop top, a big hog.

Grannie Gran used to wear an old bluish-gray robe full of holes tucked tight around her, and the way she clenched it closed still stands out in my mind. I can almost hear her walking around the hallways, up the stairs, clacking her dentures. It seemed like that house was always full of anguish, secrets, and sometimes rage. There were times when she used to keep her room door closed (when she had a certain visitor). It always felt really uncomfortable. We knew him as our uncle, because he was married to one of Grannie's sisters before she died. He and Grannie spent a lot of time together behind closed doors. When asked about it, she always said she was "greasing his hair." Until this day, the family has kept silent about it.

Marie became my safe haven and provided me with my first real consistent relationship that felt pure. I did not want to damage it in any way. If she went out and left me with a friend or Grandma Mattie, I would have these uncontrollable outbursts, where I would scream that I wanted her, I begged people to call her, and she would come home and comfort me. I don't think she had any idea what she was dealing with. She would ask me what was the matter, but I couldn't explain it. I was just terrified when she would leave me.

I remember one time when she was on the couch with a man, and the lights were dim. It was very quiet, and when I came out of the bedroom, the man seemed to be blocking my view of Marie. I thought he was doing something to her and I flipped out, because it reminded me of the feeling I had with Kent. I ran back in my room and threw a fit, screaming and rolling around on the bed. Marie apologized to the man (her client) and asked him to leave, and came in to console me again. I soon understood that Marie had her office for her therapy practice at home.

I was enrolled in the local elementary school. To my surprise when I got to the school, there were only six black kids in the whole school, and they lived in a different part of Fresno. It was the first time in my life I had ever been around other children who weren't black. In fact, the only time I used to see white people was when we went downtown in St. Louis to meet Grannie's children's father, Lonnie.

It was a very difficult adjustment for me. I was called "Little Black Sambo," and that opened up a whole new set of problems.

The two white boys that lived next door baited me into believing they wanted to be my friends. They told me they had a gift for me, and I was gullible. They handed me a package covered in a Wonder bread bag. Inside was a foil package, and inside that was a dog poop sandwich on white bread. I was outraged and hurt, but looking back as an adult, I'm amazed at the trouble they went through to welcome me in the neighborhood.

I got into a lot of fights, and Marie would often have to come to school. I eventually made friends, and they used to like to come to my house after school to swim and eat and be entertained. I got into sports and became popular. I soon got used to the idea that Marie was not going to send me anywhere. `She came up with an idea for parents who liked to go out, sort of a childcare coop, with the parents partying in the living room and the kids playing together in the bedrooms. This was all right with me, because I could always have Marie (my "Rebe") close by me.

LIFE ON SPENCER AVENUE

When I was fourteen years old, Marie asked me how I would feel if she took some more kids in. I'm not sure how I felt, or whether I answered, but it happened. Our lives changed. I think Lola, Bebe, and Angel all came together. They were sisters, daughters of Marie's brother Harry. If I thought I had emotional problems when I came, you should have seen the crew behind me.

Lola was a year younger than me, but most people thought she was the oldest. She certainly was the strongest physically. She loved to fight! I caught many blows not letting her have her way, or keeping her from beating the heck out of somebody else. Mommie Dearest would take our allowance as punishment for fighting. It didn't matter if we made up later, she still wouldn't give it back. It's funny though, we fought all the time, until we were about sixteen, and then we would go out together on double dates. We began to appreciate our friendship and freedom. One of our favorite sayings back then was "Tennis Shoe Pimp," which was our code for condoms. People generally thought Lola was the dangerous one when it came down to disagreements, but in actuality, I was the one to watch out for. Despite her rough exterior and her readiness to fight, when the Lord came into her life, after alcoholism and crack addictions, she has become so soft spoken and gentle, she became "tenderized." She is now very attentive to other people's needs.

Angel was a piece of work! She was so nervous and antsy; she had very little self-esteem. Like many of us in the family, her weight was a continuous battle, even as a child. The folks in St. Louis liked to compare her to Bebe, and this was unfair, because it made Angel self-conscious and insecure. She would rattle on and on in endless conversation, which reminds me now of my mother Brenda. Marie and Angel just couldn't make it work. Angel eventually moved into the Smith family home in Marin City. She found a place to be herself.

Marie, better known as "Mommie Dearest," tried so hard with Crystal, the fifth girl to arrive, but her technique of "mind science" didn't work with this girl. By this time, it was five of us living with her, and she was too busy to do in-depth one-on-one counseling with all of us. The fights among us were endless. We had a live-in nurse called Tilly for Grandma Mattie, who was quadriplegic and needed around-the-clock care. Tilly would call Marie several times a day saying, "*They're at it again!*" I was always in the middle, taking Crystal's side against the three sisters, not because I thought she was right, but it just seemed fair. Nobody else stood up for her. I had to hold her down from her violent outbursts against the others. It was *crazy*. There were fights constantly, with the sisters all on one side against Crystal and me.

Bebe was everybody's pride and joy. She was still so innocent and teachable when she arrived. I remember this blue checked dress that had a white apron on it, and she would love to wear that dress and pose like a little princess. We used to play dirty tricks on her sometimes. It was Christmas and we got five boxes, each smaller than the other, and we put them inside one another. She began to open box after box, and when she got to the last box, she found a stick of gum. It wasn't her real present, though. We had bought her a pair of pants and a scarf.

Another time I came to Sausalito and I used my key, thinking no one was home. I went downstairs into the old bedroom I used to sleep in, and Bebe was standing there dressed in a safari fatigue skirt with splits in it, looking like Jane in Tarzan. I took one look at her, started laughing, and said, "Whoever's in the closet, come out!" After about three minutes, this light-skinned, handsome guy stepped out, wearing only his pants. *Hmmmm*, I thought to myself.

She was so scared that I was going to tell. I looked at the two of them and I said, "All I want to know is where is the tennis shoe pimp?" She had nothing to say. Later she made an appointment to take care of business and be safe. About a week later, I got a phone call from Marie summoning me to the court at the dining room table. I didn't know what was going on; I just knew Mother told me to come home. Bebe had gone to the hospital with female problems, so Marie found out she was sexually active. I guess Bebe told her that I took her to the clinic, but what she failed to tell her was before taking her to the clinic, I had caught her playing jungle games. Marie blamed me for the whole mess, and I just ate it. Ain't that what sisters do?

I remember another story that had to do with discipline. Although I never got any whuppings, Marie soon learned that a heavier hand was going to be necessary with the new crew. One time Bebe and Crystal played hooky from school, and I knew about it. Of course, I snitched. Ain't that what sisters do? Marie was sitting at the brown grand piano, hitting keys like she knew what she was doing. As the girls walked in the door, she continued to bang away, saying, "Good evening ladies. How was school?"

She sent me downstairs to my room so I didn't get to hear all of the conversation, but I heard her tell the girls to meet her downstairs for a whupping. We could hear Marie in the room scolding them and spanking them. Mind you, these girls fought rough and tough. I believe Marie was screaming at them louder than she was hitting them. Lola, Angel, and I were busting up—if this was a whupping, she could give me one every day. It didn't compare to the mind science I got whupped with. She would kill me with "the benefit of the doubt." After Marie left the room, Bebe and Crystal came into the room with us and we all had a good belly laugh. Marie heard us and got mad again, and now this is where the real punishment started. She had Crystal and Bebe stripping floors, cleaning the baseboards, scrubbing stuff, waxing and buffing. It wasn't so funny then. Marie had discovered another new and effective way of punishment, until we got older and had our boyfriends to help us do the work (Bebe's specialty).

This whole parenting thing with so many challenged children was difficult for her. In those days, good mothers had an image to live up to, but she also had a demanding job at UCSF. Something had to give. She soon learned to delegate responsibilities. She started with cooking. At first, she used to cook all of our meals. Sometimes she would come right home from work and cook. Then she cooked whole meals for the week on Saturdays and froze them. That was harder than cooking every day.

One day she decided that each one of us was going to take a day in the kitchen. At first, we didn't know what to expect. Nobody really wanted to do it, but we had to eat. I liked cooking fried salami. The person who came up with the most interesting meals was Bebe. Every Thursday she would have some form of chili con carne. Some days with beans, some days with nachos, some days with rice. But you'd better believe it was some form of chili. We learned to create meals. Believe me, experience is the best teacher; in fact, I used the same techniques with my own daughters. Not only am I a pretty good cook today, Lola cooks and bakes for a living, and she's more than good!

Today I look back on it and I want to say that Marie had her hands full! She was a real trooper. I would have packed up all those ghetto gals and their stuff and sent them right back where they came from! The sisters kept a lot of conflict going, but it was kid stuff, which passes. I tried to keep the peace and show them how things were supposed to work since I had lived with Marie the longest, and I knew how she was. I taught them to be very careful so we didn't end up in a 3 a.m. family conference. But Crystal was so violent and full of rage she was dangerous. She could be triggered easily, and fought not like a child but like an insane adult. She would pull knives, throw hammers, and we would have to wrestle her down and take things out of her hands. It was not easy to calm her down. I figured the best thing was to hide sharp objects from her, and for years, I saw sharp objects as weapons. Today I walk by the sharp objects as a statement to myself that I am no longer ruled by that fear, or the past. Only the hammer and screwdriver are still hidden. I was still growing.

I had only seen Marie in two relationships—one was long distance, the other was with a man named John. He was an auto mechanic who became her boyfriend. He was tall and slender, and a lot of fun to be around. Most importantly, he never said anything or touched me inappropriately. I liked that! He was one of my first innocent relationships with a man. He taught me how to drive a car at age twelve—our little secret and that was the only secret that we had. I always felt comfortable with him, even when I realized he and Marie were having sex.

Marie would go to his house and spend the night, but she would check on us regularly. She would always say that a woman needed a handyman, and I always kept that in mind.

One night it was late when Marie came home. She looked a little bizarre, with her hair kind of wild, with a blasé attitude, and her striped dress was on inside out and backwards! The tag was under her chin. I was outraged! I felt she should at least have taken the time to come home like she left home. When I mentioned it to her, she pulled an MSW (Masters of Social Work) on me, and that was the night we had a discussion about sex. She steered the conversation off of herself, and onto me. I had been somewhat promiscuous already, but wasn't very experienced. She also began to talk to me about birth control. However, she was—a little late! I had already been to the clinic at Planned Parenthood, but of course hadn't told her.

I had a boyfriend named Kelo who was from Honduras. One night we went to Marin City hills, now called the Headlands, and we parked and talked. Somehow, the subject of sex came up. Kelo pulled a condom out of his wallet. I was upset at first, feeling that he had assumed I would have sex with him. He argued that he had had the condom a long time and he just wanted to be careful. We weren't worried about AIDS yet, just babies. We decided to get into the back seat. I didn't know what to do, since I was basically still a virgin. He acted like he knew what to do, but he had trouble putting the condom on, and things didn't quite pan out. In fact, later on he confessed that he was a twenty-two year old virgin, but he soon learned what to do. We began having regular sex, which we both enjoyed. Then I found pictures of him with other women, and I realized he was enjoying sex with more than just me. At first I fought to hold on to him, but the heartache was too unbearable, so after a few explosive episodes, we broke up.

Speaking of explosive relationships, when I was about seventeen, Marie met the Golden Gate Bridge Bum, also known as Ruso. One day I came home from high school, to find that Marie had a male guest; it was a man, and this was unusual. He moved in the day she met him, as far as I knew. In fact, she moved him into her bedroom. *Now what was that about,* I wondered. She had changed from being a role model and a woman of standards into someone who just allowed things to go crazy. I know that raising five girls was really difficult, but she had always protected us. She never allowed any men to say a harsh word to us, or put their hands on us. I was never a victim of Ruso's behavior, but Lola and Crystal suffered his physical abuse.

I remember one night at three o'clock in the morning. Marie woke us all up—it was family meeting time. This wasn't unusual. If she had something to say, she would gather us in the wee hours and sit us around the dining room table, and we would have a family conference. This time it included Ruso.

She didn't know he was going to be the subject; she didn't want to see what was going on. She had her own agenda about respecting one another and communicating our feelings, both positive and negative. We took this as an opportunity to tell her about how Ruso was picking fights with us and talking to us in ways that had never happened before. Ruso got upset. We got upset, and the conversation got out of control. Ruso called Lola a b——.

We all looked at Marie. She said nothing. She did nothing. It was the first time I felt unsafe with her.

A couple weeks later, he and Lola were fighting in one of the downstairs bedrooms. I looked in the room and saw him doing some karate moves on her, which he was well trained in. The room was in chaos. I ran upstairs to get Marie. I don't remember if she came down to look or not. Again, there was no repercussion behind his behavior. We kids always got repercussions for bad behavior, but he did what he wanted and she had no say. Marie then went away on a trip without resolving anything, leaving Ruso there with us, and I packed my bags and went to Marin City to stay with my cousin Dante. I loved Marie dearly, and knew that she had sacrificed her own life to take care of all these kids who weren't even hers. If she really wanted this relationship, I didn't want to stand in the way. I left her a big picture of Jesus on a cross, and on the back of it I wrote a note, telling her I loved her and wanted her to be happy, and I was leaving so that she could be happy.

When she returned home, she didn't try to make me come back. She let me be in my own adventure, which lasted about a year. Now I wish that she had tried to rescue me. Perhaps at that time, I would have let her. I returned on my own after finding out I needed to have brain surgery for a tumor. By this time, Ruso was gone. I had heard from the other family members that he had beat Marie up. I came to see her, not knowing if I wanted to see her to gloat, or out of concern for her. When I saw her with a huge black eye and a scarf tied around her head,—as if that eye could be hidden,—I felt so bad. But I was glad he was gone. She seemed quiet and humble, perhaps a lesson well learned.

I had a benign tumor on my pituitary gland and was scheduled for an operation. Grannie Gran came out from St. Louis, and she and Marie took me to the hospital. I was disappointed because my boyfriend at the time, Kelo, didn't show up. I know I had broken up with him two days earlier, but I was having brain surgery and he didn't even come to see me!

The surgery went well, and I woke up to find Grannie Gran standing over me smiling. All the feeling in my face was numb. I remember screaming, "They took my teeth!" But Grannie Gran explained to me that they were still there. Everything was just numb and swollen from the surgery. After going home, I wanted to be independent, but my head hurt so bad I couldn't raise it off the pillow. I had to ask for help with everything. I began to feel like a burden. One day I crawled out of bed and upstairs on all fours, just to go get a glass of milk. I had made a decision that I was going to stand up and lick this thing.

In two weeks, I was on the dance floor. "Disco Queen 1978" was what they called me. One night I was out at a party in San Rafael, and after partying, I realized I had locked my keys in the car. Guess who I had to call? Mommie Dearest! She was most upset, but she did come to the rescue.

At the time, I believe all the partying was about trying to get over how Kelo had treated me. Earlier that day, he had come over to Marin City and found me at a friend's house. He demanded that I go with him back to my house, so I did. When we got there we argued, but then we ended up having sex. This time it was different. He was rough and abusive, pinning me down and acting like he wanted to hurt me. This would be the last time he would touch me. He acted like he was jealous that I was over at "Pretty Boy's" house, but that was none of his business, since—we were broken up. He didn't want me, but he didn't want anybody else to have me either. In the confusion of our argument that followed the sex, I broke the window to the car he was driving, which happened to be his new girlfriend's car. He was furious, but he just drove off. This time it was really over! So I went back to the party at the club.

ON MY OWN

Being rebellious, I had left Sausalito and moved to San Francisco to live with Charles in the heart of the Tenderloin. One afternoon I woke up to find him sticking a needle in his arm. I couldn't believe my eyes! It was the first time I ever saw someone shoot drugs. I asked him what he was doing.

He explained to me, "You might as well know now; I shoot drugs. And I also sell pills." This was a huge warning sign, but I was so desperate for attention that I settled for crumbs. Most of the people around us thought that I was also going to shoot drugs, but I never did. I hate needles. As the saying goes, "I would shoot *you* before I would shoot drugs!" I would make him and his friends shoot up in the bathroom, and somehow I felt separate from it. Also, I couldn't bear to watch it.

At this time, two important changes came into my life: drugs, and my first pregnancy. I had only had one encounter with powder cocaine before my pregnancy. It was the eighties, and cocaine was hot. My heavy drug use was to happen later. I had met Charles one Friday night at a club called the Palladium. I was drawn to his luscious lips and his sexy fox-like body. He called me, and I went to visit him. He was living in a room on Sixth Street. I knew he was the kind of guy Marie would not like. However, at the time, Marie and I had been disagreeing and arguing a lot, and I was ready to declare my independence. After only two months, I was pregnant. *Welcome to independence.*

I realize now that my unconscious thoughts and feelings color my conscious perceptions. When I told my mother Marie about my first pregnancy, at first she was very disappointed. For starters, I wasn't married, I had no gainful employment, and I was only twenty years old.

Her exact words were: "Why are you putting the cart before the horse!?" She then wanted to know why I wasn't going to marry Charles.

I told her he was not the marrying kind!

She replied, "How is he good enough to have a child by, and not good enough to marry?"

My reply was sincere. "I don't know!"

In any case, she was a supportive mother, coming to the hospital to see the baby when he was born and even buying baby things for us. My son, Charles Preston Jefferson Jr., was born in September of 1979, weighing about two pounds. He was two months early.

Baby Charles had to stay in the hospital for four months. He was small and needed to be on oxygen all the time. I was there every day. I learned to work the machines, and I dressed and bathed him. I became a "hospital mom." Finally, the day arrived when I could take him home. He weighed four and a half pounds, but they let me take him home anyway. We had moved to a one-bedroom apartment next door to Charles' mother. In fact, she had arranged for us to get the apartment. Neither of us had a job, but I was determined to make the relationship work. There were all kinds of signs that this family was doomed, and my mom Marie was right, but I didn't want to admit it. I was in too deep to quit.

The baby was very important to me, perhaps for the wrong reasons, but I didn't know it until it was too late. I thought that having a child with Charles would make him a different person, but instead he became worse. I thought he would stop using drugs, stop going to jail, get a job, and live in a fantasy world with me. Unfortunately, that didn't happen. Something worse did.

I didn't know how to be a parent. In fact, I separated myself from my family because I knew that I was not living in the way they would approve. I created distance that lasted many years.

One morning I woke up to hear Charles, the baby's father, screaming. I looked at him and he was holding Charles Jr. in his arms. The baby lay there lifeless. He had passed away in the night, and we later learned it was crib death. I was so upset. I now realize the baby wasn't just a tie between us to hold us together, but he was my baby and he was gone. Charles called 911, and they came quickly, but it was too late. His little body lay in the white bassinet. It suddenly reminded me of a casket, and I never bought another one. I always used portable cribs after that.

I called Marie, and she came to my rescue—just like when I was a kid. She made all the arrangements and paid for the funeral. He was buried in a beautiful, small, powder blue pearl casket. Since the day I buried my son, I have never returned to the burial site. It was such a deep experience with death that I made a decision never to return to anyone's gravesite after the burial. It feels like opening a wound.

Marie asked me if I wanted to come home with her. This was my opportunity to walk away from my life with Charles and not look back. Perhaps it was my pride, ignorance, I don't know, but this time I didn't let her rescue me. I thanked her for all she had done and *repaid* her kindness by staying with him.

Later that night, Charles had some friends over, and someone put out a plate and put a big pile of cocaine on one side and heroin on the other. This would be my second time using cocaine. That night I also took my first and only snort of heroin. Immediately being confused and dazed, I didn't like the feeling of heroin. It was too much nodding. I felt like it was an unsafe drug for a woman, who always needs to be aware of those around her and what they're doing.

Unfortunately, I took a hold to the feeling that cocaine gave me. Before long, there were piles of cocaine on plates regularly. I think I was trying to handle the pain of the loss of my son. I felt guilty, that somehow it was my fault that the baby died. Perhaps if I had chosen a better father, or waited longer to get pregnant, or taken better care of the baby—maybe I had been too impatient or didn't feed him properly or didn't show him enough kindness?—or was I too rough?....or were we just horrible parents? To this day, I still have doubts and guilt about my child's death. It wasn't until I was able to receive the forgiveness that only God offers that I was able to move on from the doubt and guilt surrounding my son's death.

I had made an acquaintance with a girl who lived a couple of doors down named JJ. We became instant friends, and we would help each other with chores, shopping, and sharing food. After Charles and I got evicted from the apartment, JJ offered to let me stay with her. Charles had to find somewhere else to stay. This was the time when cocaine really took a hold of me.

JJ knew a lot of people with businesses, and they would come over, everybody would put in some money, and someone would go get a plateful of cocaine. In those days, we were just snorting it. I didn't really know what I was doing; I was just following the crowd. This was somewhat unusual for me, since I was usually a leader instead of a follower. In high school, friends drank and smoked weed, but I didn't participate. I was the one in control then.

I would go into Mommie Dearest's liquor supply and pour a mayonnaise jar full of vodka, and take it to school. The kids would be lit in class, and nobody was the wiser. But I didn't like the effects of alcohol, or the taste, so I didn't drink. Not then.

One day I came to the house, and JJ said, "I got something to show you!" I was curious, so I followed her into the room. She taught me just how to work it so that as I did as she said, I got a head rush that made me feel like I was on top of the world! The bliss was indescribable. I'd never felt that kind of feeling before or since. For years, I chased that high, but now I know it's just like my pastor George Lee said, "A rush from the light into the dark." It was also very erotic. I knew I wanted to do it again. Soon, it became a daily part of my life. Freebasing had arrived, but it proved not to be free.

JJ never taught me, or her boyfriend, how to cook cocaine. He came in one day, and she wasn't there; he asked me if I would cook the rock. I told him I didn't know how, but together we put the powder in the bottle, added water and heated it, but it wouldn't "rock." We heard her coming through the door, and dumped it all down the sink. We looked at each other and said, "Damn!" We never mentioned it again. Later, I learned that you had to add another ingredient, and I soon became a pro and did all the cooking for other people.

Soon after Charles and I had moved into our second apartment, JJ called me up and was very angry. She accused me of stealing her gold chain. I asked her what would I do with a gold chain, and she said, "Sell it." I told her I did not steal her chain. However, I was feeling guilty about a package of cocaine in her refrigerator that I had taken a couple of days ago before. I don't know what made me do that. She was my friend. However, I was insulted that she would accuse me of stealing a gold chain. The funny thing about it, when I got the cocaine home, it was orange, which means it was unsellable. However, I used it anyway. I wanted to tell her, but I couldn't. I thought at the time maybe her sister had taken her chain, but she probably thought her sister had taken the cocaine.

The other possibility was the boyfriend, because he became strung out too.

JJ and I were still friends after this, but we became distant. We would see each other, but we didn't really hang out together. Eventually we lost contact, and she moved to LA, cleaned up, and had a second child. Many years later, she came through the church I was attending. She was an evangelist. Not all of us were survivors, though; many of those prosperous business owners, from restaurant owners to car wash proprietors to plumbers, ended up broke, and homeless. She apologized for introducing me to the pipe. I told her there were no hard feelings. She had no idea what she was doing, and neither did I. JJ went on to become a pastor of a church in LA.

Charles Sr. and I continued to stay together, and I purposely became pregnant again within four months. I wanted this child more than ever, but not for the same reasons as before. This time I just wanted to be able to love somebody, and they would love me back unconditionally. During my pregnancy, Charles went back and forth to jail, but this gave me time to bond with my unborn baby. I knew that I wanted the baby, but I wasn't so sure about my relationship with Charles. However, I continued to visit him in jail, and took lunches to him in his work furlough program.

When he got out of jail, he didn't come home right away. After about a week, when he finally came home, he was broke and tired from his drug run, but I was still in denial and didn't want to face the problems. I continued to try to make the relationship work. We became intimate, and when I went to my regular prenatal appointment, the doctor informed me that I had a case of gonorrhea. The doctor told me that my child could be born blind and have many complications. I was furious and hurt. I felt like he put my baby and me in danger.

I waited angrily for him to come home. When he came in, I

yelled at him, telling him about my visit with the doctor, and he tried to deny that he gave me a disease. He tried to make me believe that *I* had been the one fooling around, which I hadn't! We both went to the doctor, and he tested negative. He neglected to tell me that he had been taking antibiotics. He already knew he had it, but he didn't have the courage to tell me. I couldn't help but wonder did he even care about me? Or the baby? I got treated of course, but my feelings for him were changing. We eventually moved to a one-bedroom basement apartment, and we became the parents of a daughter, Kara.

Shortly after her birth, Charles became violent for the first time. I remember we were in the garage, and we were talking about his drug use, and—his not coming home. I raised my voice in anger, and he slapped me across the face. I was in shock. The violence happened regularly over the next two months. My child was about three months old, and I knew I couldn't handle getting beat up. I had to plan my getaway. Friends and family were asking me what was I going to get for Mother's Day. I told them, "Freedom!" I waited in anticipation for the right moment to leave. I was so afraid for me and Kara.

I went to the grocery store. I had left the baby with him. When I returned, I noticed she was very quiet. At first, I thought it was just the tension in the air, so I just tried to keep the peace. Somehow, Charles and I ended up in another argument, which got very dangerous. He pulled out a knife and began to rant and rave. This time it was different. He had never pulled a weapon on me before. I didn't panic. Being the daughter of a social worker, I knew it was time to use some reverse psychology. So I began to say things to him that he wanted to hear, that I loved him, and we were just going through some bad times., and "You don't really want to hurt me; let's just lay down and relax—" He raised the knife up and stabbed it into the top of the dresser. The whole dresser shook. I took a silent deep breath, and we lay down.

After a couple hours of sleeping, I awoke to a smash against my nose! He was saying, "What the hell are you thinking about?"

I had no idea what he was talking about. Again, I didn't panic. This was the moment I had been waiting for! I began to roll around and squeeze the blood out of my nose. Then *he* panicked, and called 911. While he was letting them in, I was stuffing Kara's clothes into the diaper bag. I knew I wasn't coming back. I thought, *I'll take a whupping to walk.*

The paramedics took me to the hospital. I refused to let anybody else hold the baby—even Charles. While the doctor was examining me, I made a phone call to my Auntie Cedra. I asked her if she would come and get us from the hospital. I told her I was leaving Charles. She said she would.

Kara and I went out the back door of the Emergency Room, hoping to avoid Charles. Unfortunately, he was there at the back door, so I pretended that I was going with him. As we walked back through the long dark hospital corridor, I held Kara so tightly. I was scared to death. I didn't say a word to him until we got to the front where there were some policemen.

I looked at him and said, "You know I'm not going with you, don't you?" He looked stunned. By that time, my Auntie Cedra was waiting for me in the parking lot. I walked away from Charles and left with Auntie Cedra.

After telling my aunt about my situation, she swore I would go back. I told her all I needed was to be away from him for two weeks. When I went back to get my stuff, I found him living with a transvestite.

IGNORANCE IS A CHALLENGE

It was my twenty-first birthday. It was the beginning of a completely new phase, and it began with a dare. Lola and I were partying at the Ritz Club in San Francisco in the Tenderloin. Her brother Hawk was the DJ, so we could do just about anything we wanted. We were *young, fine, and promiscuous* and loved a good game of Truth or Dare. Lola dared me to go talk to this older man at the end of the bar. I had seen him around, but I wasn't interested in him. She said he was always asking about me, and I told her he was old enough to be my daddy's daddy. But then, she dared me. I had to do it!

I casually went over to him and introduced myself. He acted tough and cool, but I knew he was interested. He asked me if I wanted a drink. I told him I would have just one, but then I had to leave for a date. I also mentioned it was my twenty-first birthday, and he said he'd like to hang out with me. I told him at the stroke of midnight to meet me at the bar, and have a bottle of champagne. He said, "Okay."

I finished my drink and went out with the most boring man I had ever met. Marlowe took me to dinner, but I couldn't wait to get away from him. He was a really nice guy, but *that* didn't turn me on. I was wild and adventurous and liked a challenge.

Dinner was over by ten, and I went home and got dressed up for my midnight rendezvous. I got back to the bar, and Lou was there. and guess what? *He* was the one who had my bottle of champagne. I explained to him that if I was drinking with him, I would expect him to get me home safely. He agreed. We drank the bottle and then we started on my favorite drink, a Singapore Sling. It was—a mixture of vodka, gin, rum, syrup, and orange juice, with a cherry on top.

I did a lot of dancing and a lot of drinking; in fact—I got very drunk. He made sure I got home safely. I woke up the next morning, and he was lying beside me. We hadn't done any drugs that night, and I didn't know then that he was a dealer. He was known as Red Cap on the street. We began a relationship that would last for years.

Although, I had experience selling cocaine from the house, he soon taught me how to sell it on the streets. He showed me how to recognize quality product and how to cut it; in other words, I became Mrs. Cap and a full-fledged dealer, at a time when most women were not allowed to be dealers. He taught me how to be a "Lady in the Game" and educated me on the fine points of being a female dealer. I never compromised, never used with suppliers—unless Lou was there with me and gave his approval. The big suppliers would sell to me while he was in jail, of course with his permission by phone, but when he got out, the suppliers cut me off.

A lot of customers would come to our house to buy and/or indulge with us. We would go through ounces a night. It started off as fascinating and exciting, and ended up in ruins. When he and I were getting packages ready, I would use some of the old skimming tactics that JJ taught me. As I would be folding the packages, I was sitting on the opposite side of the table, and I would be dropping packages on the floor, and sticking them later in my sock. I had my own little business on the side. When he went to work, customers would come to me. I got away with this for a long time.

Then one day he said, "Is something wrong with your ankle?"

"No," I said with an innocent face and a pounding heart.

He said, "Let's see."

I was busted. For a while, he wouldn't let me come out and smoke with him and the customers. That was all right with me, since I had my own stash.

After that though, I had to find another avenue to supply my growing habit. He kept his stash in a brown locked suitcase. I soon learned that I was a locksmith.

I actually made a key that would unlock his suitcase. In the beginning, I would unlock it, cut the dope, put it back, and lock it up. I got away with this for a long time, but as my habit progressed, I would unlock the suitcase, but there was no putting it back. He came home one day, unlocked his suitcase, and saw…nothing!

I had smoked up the whole suitcase. He was furious. He yelled, and screamed, and lectured me, but to my surprise, he did not hit me. He called one of his suppliers, got some credit, and sent me to work selling drugs. During these years, I liked variety, and was quite promiscuous. *Why should I give up my independence?* I continued to see Stuart once a month and got pregnant with Jerri, who turned out to be Lou's child. Later on, some time after Jerri's birth, I got pregnant again, had my first miscarriage, and once again became pregnant. I was busy. Lou had planted the idea in my head that if a woman came up pregnant, the baby belonged to the man she was living with.

The history of Deena's conception is the story of me in one of my lower forms of self and selfishness. For a time I was sleeping with both Lou and Stuart. Deena was conceived in confusion. I was seeing Stuart, whose sister married into the family. and I called her Auntie Jo. Stuart and I got together on a fluke. His girl was pregnant, and I was at a club where he was. We realized we had a little chemistry. I went to the phone booth, called Auntie Jo, and asked her if she would mind if I dated Stuart. She said no. So we started sneaking around and stealing moments when his girl wasn't looking. I was at their house with Kara every weekend. Stuart had a lot of women but that didn't matter to me because I was not looking for a man. I was looking for a good time, and he was a good time. This lasted several years.

He set himself up. The thought never occurred to me that the baby was Stuart's, even if it was. That was the game.

Years later, about in 1989, Stuart dropped by my job at Glide Memorial, and we ended up at his hotel. We tried to rekindle a moment from the past, but it didn't work. I was thirty now. He didn't make me feel sixteen again, and I told him so. We kissed and said goodbye.

FROM ONE MAN TO ANOTHER

The day I met Jon Pierre, I was working at Church's Chicken on Seventh and Market in San Francisco. I had just been released from serving a four-month sentence in San Bruno County Jail for two direct sales of controlled substances to police. I went from making an income of two thousand dollars a week to seventy dollars a week at Church's. Considering the circumstances, I wasn't mad! Each conviction carried fifteen years, but that was my first time being arrested for anything.

I wrote a letter to the judge explaining my situation (I've always been crafty!) I told him that I had gotten involved with the wrong crowd, and that I was just supporting my own habit and not dealing, and that I wanted to change. He took pity on me and gave me a lenient sentence of four months, with two years probation.

Jon was also an employee of Church's Chicken, though I could never figure out what his duties were. He would be washing the windows, then would disappear. After a few hours he would reappear on the other side of the building, still washing windows. At first, I had no attraction to him, which was strange. He became my friend and would bring me lasagna for lunch; he was somebody I could talk to. God knows I needed a friend. Lou was in jail on another drug charge, and unfortunately, he was going to be away for a while.

The Filipino family I was living with at the time, who were friends of Lou's, and fellow cocaine users, started out being nice to me. We would all get high together, including the dog, who would lick his pile of cocaine off the carpet. One time when I was reprimanded to the court unexpectedly, I called home to let them know I wouldn't be coming home for a while. I told them I had hidden an eighth of cocaine somewhere in the house. The dog found the stash I had hidden, sniffing it out in the flowerpot. It was gone by the time I got out, and so was Lou. He was kind enough to let me know where his hidden stash was, thinking I was crazy enough to go back to selling. I went and retrieved it from the hotel he was busted at, and smoked up the whole two ounces. When he asked about it, I told him I didn't find it.

As time went on, money was tight for all of us. I was no longer dealing, after doing the time in jail, and the family had no more resources left. They finally asked me to leave, and I had no idea where I was going to go.

I shared this information with Jon. He suggested that I move in with him. I told him I couldn't possibly do that because my boyfriend, Lou, would not understand. So Jon decided we should take a trip to the San Francisco Jail and explain it to him. So we did. Of course, he wasn't happy, but Jon sat down and told him that I was in a bad position, and he really wanted to help me. In fact, Jon said that I was "damaged goods," meaning that I was pregnant.

The truth is that I wasn't sure who the father of this baby was. I had been with Lou, as well as I had slept with a man who was an old boyfriend of my cousin. I was mad at her because I heard she called child protective services on me about my children. I also had an affair with a guy I met in County Jail who could play the saxophone. That was my only attraction to him, but he didn't live up to the horn, so that was quickly over. Therefore, I had three baby-daddy possibilities. I had already told Lou I was pregnant, and that it might not be his. What was he prepared to do? He told me he would never look at the bastard. I told him that the relationship was over.

I moved in with Jon in his two-bedroom Sunnydale project. I was curious to know why he had a two-bedroom apartment. He told me he had two children that lived with their mother, but they only came to visit him every other weekend. The house was a mess. But who was I to complain? At first, he was very nice to me. He would comfort me like a brother, and we were not involved romantically—yet.

I had decided to abort the child. I felt like there were too many ill feelings around it, and it wouldn't be fair to the child. Jon took me to my appointment. We had circled the place several times before we went in. I asked him why we were walking around, and he said he knew I was nervous and he wanted me to take time to think it over.

He said, "I'm going to mention this one time, and I'll never mention it again. You can have this baby, and I'll raise it as mine."

But I said, "No." We went in for the appointment. He was against it; he told the receptionist that he was not the father, as if to distance himself from me. I think he felt that abortion was wrong.

As I walked out of the clinic after the abortion, Jon was there to accompany me home. I could actually feel where the baby had been inside of my womb. It was empty. For a while, I was devastated. I was slowly able to forgive myself. I knew this was not the time to take on the burdens of another child.

In a few months of living together, Jon and I became involved. My kids were now living with my Auntie Cedra. Kara was five, Jerri was three, and Deena was under one. I was visiting them regularly and they also came to stay with me on the weekends. They got along well with Jon's two children, Marsha and Kawan. In fact, they became brothers and sisters, and to this day, some of them still communicate with each other. I became their second mother.

We were lying on the bed, which we did often, talking about his latest conquests, or whatever I was going through. Then all of a sudden, he was on top of me. At first, it seemed okay, but then we both agreed that we didn't want to do this. He got up and left, and I lay there and thought about it. Soon the attraction got stronger, and we decided we would try, just once, to have sex. The night we decided to have sex, we were all involved and enjoying each other, and suddenly there was a knock at the door.

We asked, "Who is it?" We were not prepared for the answer. It was Lou.

We both panicked. I ran upstairs while he ran around picking up evidence. I was amazed at how calm Jon acted. He was so welcoming to Lou, he even invited him to stay with us. Lou, being the hustler he was, took him up on his offer. This was going to be complicated, because Jon had his two kids coming to stay, and I had my three daughters coming to stay on weekends, so now I had five kids and two boyfriends! I had already made the decision that I didn't want to be with Lou any more, but I had not told him yet. I really didn't want to have sex with him, but this was his first night out, and he was ready. I was standing at the top of the stairs and looked downstairs at Jon's face, and I knew he was upset.

He left for a few hours. I took this time to tell Lou that my feelings for him had changed, but I hadn't wanted to send him a Dear John letter. I also explained to him that this would be the last time that he touched me, and then we went ahead and had sex. He thought I didn't want to be with him because of Jon, but I told him that wasn't true.

"I got me a spot downtown. Are you coming with me?" Lou asked.

"No," I said. "I don't like that lifestyle any more." Jail had changed me, I thought.

"Well, I'm gonna keep doing what I do until the police tell me I can't do it no more," Lou said.

"I can't believe you just gave up your job at the phone company to sell drugs and pimp women," I said bitterly. Lou soon moved out into a hotel room in the Tenderloin. My friend Boss took me by a bar on Eddy Street to see Lou. I needed some money, and he was always good for a few dollars. I asked Boss to wait in the car while I went in. I was shocked to see Lou sitting and talking with Jon. I turned around before they saw me and left. I asked Boss to take me to a church.

We found a little Catholic Church open, and I went in by myself and sat for a long time. I asked God what was wrong with me. *What should I do?* It gave me comfort for a minute. But then I was my old hustling self. Boss gave me some money and dropped me at home. Later when Jon came in, he had cocaine. I asked him where he got it, and he said, "Lou gave it to me so I would leave you alone. He even offered me money to put you out, so you would go back to him."

I went to see Lou at his hotel room, and he tried to bribe me with drugs, money, and oral sex, to come back to him. I refused. I did take the drugs and money though. Jon was starting to reveal his true self, that—he too was an undercover IV drug user and he liked to use cocaine. Everyone around me was starting to smoke crack or shoot up.

I eventually became pregnant with my son Jason, and now we had a common bond. Then drama really began.

IT'S ALL ABOUT THE MONEY

The year was 1988, and it was a cool, brittle night. I had just let Lou take Jerri and Deena to Flint, Michigan to visit his family, who had never met the girls before. Lou and I had broken up, but we had made an agreement that if we ever broke up we would share the children equally and never use them as a weapon against each other. I was totally trusting that he would honor the agreement, even though my Auntie Cedra was against the idea.

I was distraught and decided to take a walk. I felt I needed something to relieve the pain I was feeling in my heart for the absence of my girls. I didn't have any money. As I was walking and crying, I looked up and noticed that I was standing on Octavia Street. I thought about some of the female crack users I knew and how they got money for their drugs. At first, selling myself was hard, but it also fulfilled a distorted mental desire that I had confused with a need. My need was to be touched, to be wanted, to captivate someone to be enchanted by me. Fantasy can be rewarding to the flesh.

I convinced myself that a variety of men would be pleasurable; after all, no one man was ever consistent in making me feel valuable. Most of the time I was able to choose guys that I was attracted to anyway. By charging them, I could be justified in earning money for myself.

I looked around to see if anyone was paying attention to me. What harm could it do? I thought. I had slept with a lot of guys and had nothing to show for it,—except children. Perhaps this was when I made the decision that from now on, in order for a guy to touch me, he would have to pay. Even if I wanted it!

I took a swig of my cheap wine, and I got bolder and more confident in what I was doing. All my doubts were fading away, and my addiction was calling me. Suddenly a car slid up beside me, a red Porsche with a white guy sitting in it. I knew I had to be careful of what I said or I could get arrested.

I said, "Hello."

He said, "Hello." We paused. I decided to let him lead. "What are you doing?" he asked.

"Just hanging out," I replied.

He asked, "Want to take a ride?" I was scared, and I hesitated.

I looked in his car to see if there was anything that I should be aware of, like—a gun, a rope, a shovel, or gasoline with matches. Everything looked safe, so I took a chance, and got in his car. We drove around looking for a dark, quiet place to park. We found one on the far side of the park. We were chatting, and the subject of money came up. He offered me sixty dollars for fifteen minutes of time. It sounded like a lot of money for fifteen minutes. I knew girls who would had turned tricks for a hit of crack,—or five dollars.

After the deed was done, he dropped me off in the spot where he had picked me up. He said he was pleased, and in the future, he would be looking for me. I thought about what he was saying, and wondered if he really would see me out here again. He asked me my name, and I told him Chickie, and he drove away. At first, I felt kind of dirty. What was I doing? Then I looked down at the sixty dollars in my hand, and feeling somewhat embarrassed, I took a few more sips of wine from the bottle in my purse and thought, *I'm gonna get a hit.* And I did.

As time went on, working the streets became easier and easier. I learned to be selective about the tricks I would accept. After all, the streets was a dangerous place, and no matter how careful I was, I ended up getting hurt plenty of times, raped, and even brushed death several times. I was driven by my addiction to keep going. I was hard headed.

By this time, Jon and I were homeless, and I was living with my cousin on Webster St. Someone in my family had called CPS to have Jason, my one-year-old son, removed to a foster home. One night I was at my cousin's house and there was a knock at the door. When I opened it, there were the police and a social worker. They told me I had to surrender Jason. I was shocked, and I demanded to know why. In my own mind, it was unfair because I had been clean for a couple of days, and I intended to stop using. They just said, "M'am, give us the child." I clutched him and blatantly refused to give him up. They pulled and tugged, but I wouldn't let him go.

Finally, Jon said, "Hand him to me." It was a lot easier for me to hand him to Jon than to the police. They said they got a report of abuse from a family member. I denied abusing him. Yes, I was homeless and on drugs, but I didn't think I was abusing him. I fed and changed him, and I never left him with anyone else while I was getting high. But they took him, anyway. I was humiliated, and heart broken. So much anger welled up in me that I didn't know how to cope. I thought, *What's the use? My life is never going to change. All my kids are gone. Might as well get high.*

I went back to working the streets. I never told Jon what I was up to when I left the house. I just came back with money and crack, and he didn't question it. He wanted the drugs as much as I did.

I had serious complaints about the way Jason had been taken

from me. Several days before, I had made a decision to take a look at my drug use and how it had affected my living conditions.

After CPS left with my son, I called my Aunt Cedra and asked her why she reported me to CPS when we had agreed she would take care of Kara for me until I got on my feet? She told me that when I had brought Kara to her she thought I was on something. After losing two of my children to foster care, and the other two to their father…I was a mother without purpose.

All thoughts of recovery were in the pipe. It became a "pipe dream." I spoke often about my children, but it was like a distant hope, fading faster with every hit. I had the illusion that my children gave me focus and an identity as somebody important. I sank into depression and even heavier drug use.

One day, Jon confronted me in the bathroom.

"I heard you've been workin' Octavia Street. Is it true?" he asked.

"Yes, it's true," I said.

"Why?" he asked.

"For the money," I said calmly, though my heart was pounding. "It's nothing personal. Just business."

I saw the change in his face when I said it. Perhaps he was hurt, but he knew the game. His mother was a prostitute and his father a rolling stone. In fact, he told me that he had lost his virginity to some of his mother's friends who were—also prostitutes. I told him it was just work. I kept my money for myself, but I sometimes shared my drugs with him. I didn't believe in that "pimp-ho" stuff. With my money, I also bought us groceries, clothes for the kids, medicines, and a lot of birthday parties. I would show up with birthday cakes, and gifts,—wherever my children were. The times I didn't know where they were, I still baked them a cake and celebrated their birthdays. My hustle money was supporting us.

Some of my most vivid and painful memories of those days are of myself on the empty streets at about 4 a.m. or later. Finally having made some money, I would go shopping for groceries, and with the bags tied together strapped across my shoulders, or pushing a shopping cart, I would go to my dealers and cop. I would try to make it home before the children got up. Exhausted, my feet calloused and hurting from walking all night, I still felt successful because I had *brought home the bacon.*

I still don't know how this made Jon feel. His hustling skills were minimal, and he wasn't much of a provider. I knew he was making money doing odd jobs and helping people with their computers, but he shared very little with the house.

It made me sad to see him tweaking around the house, looking for crack on the floor, or constantly scraping the residue off his empty pipe, so sometimes I would go get something for him. I called this "working a twist," which meant not just scoring drugs, but having things the way I wanted them to work out. It was a hustle, and I was good at it.

As crazy as it sounds now, I used to carry a lot of stuff with me when I went hustling. It's like my whole life was being carried in my bag. I would have my pipe, phone book, lighter or matches, condoms, and, of course, my drugs—and my Bible. I would always stop and read Bible verses on little stoops in quiet areas. I would ask God to bless my *adventure,* and help me be successful for the night. After reading, I would take a hit off my pipe. Then I'd go back to work. Even in my stupidity and suffering, I reached for God, and He still met my needs.

I had good days and bad days. Good days were when I made money and made it home safely. Bad days came along, too. One day I met a guy on Third Street who looked normal. He was a brother with deep green eyes and a gold chain. He said he wanted to smoke crack and have sex. We walked and stopped behind a train that was parked. We both took a hit of crack, and all of a sudden, the guy freaked out. He grabbed me around the neck and began choking me. We fell down on the ground. I looked in his eyes and fear came over me...he was enraged and way out of control. I was terrified, but I knew if I wanted to survive, I had better think of something quick. His chokehold on me was so tight I thought I was going to pass out. I stopped struggling, thinking this might make him calm down and loosen his grip. As I relaxed, his grip softened. I tried to stroke his ego, by smiling and caressing him. I didn't know what he wanted, but I knew it was important to try to please him somehow. Some people were walking by on the other side of the train, and although they couldn't see us, I took this opportunity to scream for help. He became frightened and let me go, then got up, and walked away.

I lay there on the ground, gasping for breath, scared and ashamed, but alive. I gathered my thoughts and checked my pockets for the money he had given me earlier. It was still there. I then ran three blocks home and told my "god-brother" Andy what had happened. I told him it was no use in going to look for him. I was sure he was gone by now. I was still pretty shaken up, so I sent Andy to score the drugs for me with the money I had made. Believe me, it was rare for me to trust anyone to cop my drugs.

Andy was someone I had met at Glide Memorial Church. We became very good friends; most people knew us as brother and sister. I usually told him about all my little secrets, and he was always comforting. Like me, Andy was on drugs, and we shared drugs together, but it wasn't the basis of our relationship. I used to see how he treated women, how he would go from one to the next.

Andy would cook, clean, and take care of the kids whenever I was out hustling, or I just wasn't home. I trusted him more than I trusted Jon, who was apparently fooling around with somebody because there were many days when he didn't come home. I remember when I found out he had moved in with another girl. I had learned this through my son. He took Jason for a night, but they spent it at the new girlfriend's house. Jason came home and told me. I was angry, hurt, and I couldn't believe that Jon was such a coward that he would use our son for his dirty work.

Leaving Jason with Andy, I went running through the streets, finding myself walking down the middle of Third Street full of confusion. I needed to get high. I also needed to come up with some money. I ran into a trick I knew as Tu, and he wanted to know what was going on. Tu was an older black man, both handsome and nuts. I never understood why he chose to live on the streets. I told him a little bit about Jon's betrayal and rejection, but comforting was not what I needed from him. We went to his spot, which was a small, homemade shack built around a big tree. It had no plumbing, no electricity, but it was cozy. I didn't like him to touch me, but I tolerated it because it was always good money. The only thing was that he would get possessive, and I would have to remind him that our relationship was purely business.

After getting the money, I returned home. Jon was gone, but Andy was there. We got high, but this time it was different. All the years that we'd gotten high together, there was nothing between us. He put arms around me, like he did so many times before, but suddenly, this time for a brief moment I saw him in a different light. I felt I needed him at the time. He wasn't sure about it, but I persuaded him. I cried through the whole thing. Afterward, we went back to our old ways of friendship, and we never talked about it.

I continued to "date" Tu regularly, maybe two or three times a week. He wanted me to get rid of Jon and be with him, but I told him that I was going to marry Jon. He said I would be ruining my life if I did. I didn't listen to him, and the wedding date was set. We were married in 1992. Jon was supposed to provide the preacher. He didn't. The maid of honor didn't show up, but another girlfriend was there. She brought food, and Budweiser, and her support—even though she knew I was making a bad decision.

Here we were in the middle of the park, which Tu had promised to decorate. I had even picked all the Pampa grass around town and stacked it for him in the park to put out for an aisle. He didn't do it. I was transitioning from my Muslim to my Baptist phase. So I wore a white head covering and a long white cotton gown, but the most important thing I had on was my chastity chain. It was made of tab tops, with a big rusty key hanging from it. It secretly symbolized my freedom of choice around my sexuality—instead of being forced. I got to decide who and when I would have sex with. With it on, I felt the power in my hands!

The only preacher in sight was my mother Marie who had a minister's license. At first she was shocked and questioned me whether I really wanted to do this. When I said yes, she seemed to get caught up in the idea of performing a wedding, and she threw herself into it. I didn't want to admit it, but I knew from the beginning marrying Jon was definitely not a wise decision, but as always, I was committed to making it work. As the Congo drums played on, I pressed on in my stubborn rebellion.

Beginning on my wedding night, Jon's absences happened more often. In the meantime, even though we were married, I continued to see Tu. I had let him rent a bedroom for a month in my house. However, we never did business there. He became more obsessive, as if I was his wife. Once, my friends and I were in the living room getting high. He came in and started ranting and raving in an aggressive way. At first, they didn't know what was up, but I said, "Oh, he just rents a room here." The guys asked what I wanted to do about him, and I told them I wanted him to leave, so they put him out with all his stuff. Tu begged me to let him have access to the back yard to store his things, and I agreed, since I needed the money.

A couple of days later he was still acting so crazy I told him to leave me alone. He wouldn't, and I warned him that I had a can of gasoline, and if he didn't stop, I was going to douse him. He didn't stop. I threw the gasoline on him. I then flicked the lighter to show him how serious I was.

I looked up and Kara, my oldest daughter, was looking out the window. I didn't want her to see me do that.

I put my lighter away and I told Tu to leave. I said I would meet him later on the corner where a group of us played drums. When I got down there, he was there waiting. I didn't want to deal with him then, I just wanted to play music, so I told him I'd meet him at his tree house. Later I went to meet him. He was belligerent as usual. I started walking away. I knew it was a mistake to come there, but I wanted the money. He followed me shouting and waving his hands. There was a white van passing by, and a police officer was in it. I flagged him down and asked him to tell Tu to leave me alone. The officer tried to tell us to go our separate ways, but Tu kept shouting and threatening the police and me. The officer got out of the van, trying to calm him down, and I was walking away, but looking back. I was saying, "Tu, you're going to die if you keep fooling with me." I saw the officer pull out his gun. I thought this would make Tu settle down, but he kept ranting and raving, then he leaped at the officer who fell down on the ground. The gun went off. Then there was silence for a minute. Tu lay on the ground, not moving.

I wanted to run. The officer, who was Latino, said, "Lady, please don't leave me like this." It could have looked like the officer shot an unarmed man for no reason.

He called for backup, and police cars raced up. Tu was lying there on the ground. I didn't see any blood, so I didn't know how badly he was hurt. I was still feeling angry with him. The police took me to the station where I was put in a room and questioned by a female officer, who was very kind to me.

After about an hour, I asked her what happened to Tu. She said, "He didn't make it." I was stunned, and felt guilty. A man was dead because of his involvement with me, and I felt responsible. The officer sensed that I was distraught, and she continued to counsel me. Later, she even became a friend.

After the police released me, I needed a hit bad. I went to the streets looking for a new trick. As I was walking, a car pulled up beside me and people started jumping out, screaming, "She's the one! That's her!" It was his family. I thought they were going to hurt or kill me. I tried to explain to them that he had tried to jump the police. We blamed each other for what had happened to Tu. That Sunday, the drumming group got together and did a tribute to him, and I played and danced like I'd never danced before.

One day I woke up and saw his shoes, his socks, his shirt, his pants, his jacket, his briefcase, but I didn't see Jon. I went through the house looking for him but he appeared to be gone. I knocked on Emma's door, (a friend we let stay in the front room with her two kids,) and I asked her if she had seen Jon. There was silence, and then she said no. I said, "Okay, I'll just wait right out here until he comes out. I know he's in there." About five minutes later the door opened, and Jon came out wearing just his boxer shorts. I asked him, "What are you doing in there? Especially in your underwear?" I could feel the tension in the air. Emma shouted out, "I don't want your man!"

"Then why is he in the bedroom with you?" I said. She made no reply. I turned back to Jon, and began to rant and rave, and all of a sudden, he hit me in the eye with his fist. Everything got quiet. I asked Emma to leave, but I should have asked him. I acted like I didn't have a clue, but I had known that he had been disappearing with her when she lived down the street. The problem was that I felt he was cheating on me, but I was desperate to keep the relationship going, fearing the unknown of being alone.

The next day my eye was black and blue, and my whole face was swollen. I was embarrassed and ashamed to show my face to my children, especially Kara. I knew she was being affected by everything I was doing, but I didn't want her to see that I was hooking and doing drugs, and I particularly didn't want her to see me beaten up. But she saw it, and she knew what was going on. However, I was just stuck, and I didn't want to talk about it. Some teenaged boys that hung out at my house were coming over soon, to package their drugs and get high. I didn't want them to see me either, but I needed to get high. When they saw me, they asked me what happened, and I told them the truth. They were angry, but it was "business as usual."

It was raining that day, and after the boys left that night, I pulled the book case away from the window so the books wouldn't get wet. I found a half an ounce of uncut cocaine. I wasn't looking for anything. I decided that I would cut it and take a little, and replace it. I didn't tell Jon where I had got the dope; I just shared it with him. Unfortunately it wasn't enough, (it's never enough!) so I decided to tell him about the stash I'd found.

"Let's just take a little more, and put it back. In fact, hide it so I won't know where it is," I said. I didn't trust myself. The night went on and we partied together. The next morning Jon told me he had something to do. I told him to make sure he'd be back by the time the teenagers were there, so we could give them back their stash. Unknown to me, he had left and taken the entire stash. (Why did I trust *him?*)

Hours and hours went by. No Jon. I could feel panic building in me. The teenagers came and I told them that I'd found their stash and Jon had put it up, and he wasn't back yet. They were patient for awhile, then they started to get rowdy, setting firecrackers off in the house and acting in a very threatening manner. Eventually they left, but not before they threw the telephone out of the kitchen window, shattering glass everywhere. I was terrified for myself and my children.

I found out that Jon had gone to Sunnydale to his brother's

house, leaving me and my children alone to face the angry teenagers. A girlfriend of the teenagers came to my door and asked me to let her in. I told her I was afraid, that I didn't take the dope, and if I had, my kids and I would not still be here waiting for the teenagers. She said she understood, that she just wanted to sit down and talk to me. I opened the door, and the teenagers came rushing in, and they held me and my kids hostage.

They separated us, putting us in different rooms, and told me they were going to hurt the kids. I was hysterical, begging them not to touch the children. They made me strip down to my underwear, and I thought they were going to rape me. I could hear the kids screaming and crying. They tried to push me out the window, but I fought them and they stopped. They left the room and I followed them so I could see the kids. It appeared they were OK. The teenagers then went through the house taking everything worth anything—my typewriter, my TV, VCR, what little money there was, even the children's boxes of candy for the school fund raiser. I later found out they had held a knife to my middle daughter's throat and told the kids they were going to cut her. But they didn't. Finally, they left. I sat there holding my kids.

Jon came home broke and tired. He got his brother to work out some arrangements with the teenagers, but they never bothered us again. As always, I took him back, thinking I was being loyal and forgiving. He was always being deceitful, and people thought I was a part of it. He would pull scams and sometimes he would get caught, and I would take part of the blame, but he really wasn't with me or sharing the drugs with me.

My home was always open to people we knew who were homeless or having a hard time. Of course, they would pay some rent, which we needed, and I was the one who collected the money. One time we had a whole cast of characters living with us: Andy, Rooster, occasionally a man we called "Mr. Be-Back," Alley Boy, my uncle Ted Jr., and Jon's brother, who was a Muslim. Jon copied many of his Muslim ways. He would manipulate Jon and the rest of the guys in the house to give their rent money to Jon, knowing that they could all get high together and there was nothing I could do about it. I confronted Jon in front of them, and he tried to change the subject by bringing out an old electric bill, demanding to know why I hadn't paid it. He was counting on me getting defensive, one of the ways he liked to play mind games with me. It was a sport for him, and it caused me to doubt myself.

This time I didn't fall for it. I demanded the rent money. He didn't have it, so to save face in front of his brother and friends, he pulled a gun on me. At this moment, the phone rang and it was one of my regular tricks. I told him I was busy, but I would meet him soon. While I was on the phone, Jon put the gun away. I was furious that the guys hadn't tried to protect me, but later I found out they all knew the gun was empty. I told Jon's brother that I knew he was behind this situation, and also that he manipulated the guys, and that he wanted me for himself. I demanded that he get out now, or I'd call the police. He just sat there, but he knew what I was saying was the truth. Later he left.

I went to meet the trick, who still owed me money. When I asked him about it, he made up some excuse about paying me. I was caught up in the moment, shaking and moving, and I knew I needed a hit. I was having withdraws because I had not had a hit in sometime so I refused to give him what he wanted. He went in his house. I picked up a brick and broke his headlight on his car, and I left. Later he called me and asked me why I did that. His dad was going to be upset. I told him, "Tell your daddy you owe me some money for sex and you wouldn't pay me. He'll get it."

Later, I went back to see him, and apologized. He gave me some money, some dope, and I promised him some free sex for the headlight. "Take it out in trade."

As time went on, Jon and I continued in our relationship of drug addiction and abuse. The final episode of abuse took place on Egbert Street. That night I came in worn out from walking the streets. Work was scarce that night, and I didn't have much money or dope. I didn't really want to share the ten-shot I had, but I did. My uncle Ted Jr. was in the living room. I went straight into the bedroom. Jon came in, and we took a hit on the pipe. It wasn't enough to satisfy us, but—just enough to get us edgy. I saw that he was "fiending," and even though I had just come in, I would have gone back out, but he didn't give me a chance. He started an argument and he seemed fired up already. I was sitting on the bed. I was not expecting what happened next.

He straddled me and pinned my arms down with his knees, and he began beating me in my face mercilessly. I tried to fight him off, but I was pinned down. I just lay there crying and screaming. Uncle Ted Jr. never appeared. Jon kept hitting me. Finally, he got up and left. My face was bleeding. I went in to wash my face. I needed a hit. I put on some dark glasses and went back out to look for a trick. There was no relief this time. I had to come home empty-handed. I opened the door, and my uncle Ted was sitting at the piano, and he was playing and singing "Precious Lord." The song spoke to me and touched me in a deep place. I went in, lay down, and fell asleep.

The next morning I woke up, and it was dark. Then I realized my eyes were swollen shut, and electricity had been cut off. I was afraid to look in the mirror. I didn't want my kids to see me. I finally looked at myself in the mirror, and I broke out in tears. I heard my kids waking up, so I ran to the couch and lay down and pulled the covers over my head. They came looking for me, and they asked me why I had the covers over my head. I told them the truth—I had gotten beat up. They began to cry, and at that moment, I felt like the worst mother in the world. Even though I was hurting, I still needed to provide for them. I asked my uncle if he would take me to a county program to get the electricity turned back on. I couldn't see, so my uncle had to hold my hand and walk me down the street. I didn't wear sunglasses because I felt I couldn't hide anything anymore. I told the person at the county office that I had gotten robbed and beaten up. They paid for my bill.

When we returned home, Jon was there. I bypassed him and went into the kitchen to cook. A few days later, I was feeling revengeful. I hadn't called the police on him, but I went to his friends' houses and showed them what he had done to me. I wanted everybody to see what kind of man he was. They all could see it, but the problem was, I couldn't see it.

Jon was having company in the back room every day, but we were barely talking. He was constantly high, but nobody was sharing anything with me. One night after his friends left, I was in the kitchen cooking chicken, and I was holding a knife. Jon came in to confront me about showing my face to his friends. He came at me, but this time I drew the knife at him. I said I wasn't taking any more beatings. Ted Jr. ran into the kitchen and got between us. He said that was enough. I put the knife down, and Jon left. I knew at that moment if I didn't do something, I would have to tell my son that I killed his father, if he didn't kill me first.

My uncle convinced me to call the police, which I did. I didn't want to get Jon arrested, because he had told me earlier that month that he had cancer. I knew he needed help and that his behavior was out of control, (and of course so was mine, but I couldn't see it yet.) The police came, they took pictures of my face, and told me to call them the next time I saw him. When he came home, I called them. They came and got him. Like any woman who'd been a victim of domestic violence, I dropped the charges. However, in California, the district attorney will press charges regardless.

Jon got nine months in jail. Of course, I went to see him, and took the children. On Valentine's Day, I dressed up in red and white and dressed up my four kids, Jon's two kids, and two girls I took care of in red and white, and we went to visit Jon in jail. I was so hoping to be appreciated. I even wore my sunglasses so my black eyes wouldn't show. He didn't seem to notice or appreciate me or the kids all dressed up for him. I left there disappointed once again.

The following Sunday, the children and I went to visit him again. He seemed happy to see the children but not me. I asked the guard if this was a contact visit, and he said, "Yes."

I mustered up all the courage and anger I had inside, and I reached over and slapped him with full force. I screamed, "*Contact!*" and I felt full of joy and powerful in the moment. He felt embarrassed and shocked, and so did the kids. His son Kawan was angry with me for hitting his dad. The police promptly put us out, telling me that I could get locked up for that. At that moment, I didn't care. I explained to the police that he had it easy, and I had all the responsibility—and all the kids. "He deserved it!" They let me go.

SALVATION HAS COME TO MY HOUSE

I wanted to look at who I had been and the price that I'd paid for my behavior, so I went to Glide Memorial Church, where Jon was attending the Facts on Crack Program. This program was designed by Cecil Williams, to be a place where addicts could share their history, their struggles, and their ways of staying clean. Jon had graduated from the First Generation Class, and he swore that he was clean. I wanted to be clean too, but didn't know the right spiritual path for me. I felt the need to be rooted. *But where?*

Before I went to jail, I had visited one of Glide's five o'clock Recovery Meetings. It made such an impression on me that I threw my pipe in the middle of the aisle, stood up, and declared that I was through smoking crack! After the meeting, I rushed home to share this with Jon and the rest of the people who were hanging in the house. I didn't understand why they weren't rejoicing with me! I stayed clean for a whole week on one meeting. However, it is very difficult to maintain sobriety when there is smoke flying around your head. I learned later in life that when you quit doing something, you can't allow anyone around you to do it in your presence. The memory of the first meeting and Jon's saying he was clean, as well as going to Glide celebrations as a kid with Marie, all offered me an assurance that I would be able to get a new life.

Unfortunately, I sometimes live in a fantasy world, (which sometimes protects me), but it's not the real world. The program had a good concept, keeping people off the streets and facing the fact that they are addicts, but when the meetings are over, they go back to their same environment and ways of thinking and surviving. These are triggers for addiction. People exposed the most intimate details of their lives, but had no support after opening up. Then the information we revealed was used in sermons and news conferences, and it made the church look like a savior to the recovery world. However, we didn't get any ongoing therapy, and it became a show. We would dress up to look the part of clean and sober and put ourselves on display, but many of us were still using.

In fact, I was clean that first three months, but there were only three of us in the Second Generation Class. We had to repeat the class because they didn't want to graduate only three people. The crowd wasn't big enough! Andy, Bubba, and I made up graduation cards that said "3.5," since we weren't big enough to graduate on our own. We resented that. By the time I did get to graduate, I had relapsed. Jon came in one night looking kind of crazy, and I asked him what happened? He told me that he'd accidentally slipped and used, and I felt so bad for him. I thought it just wasn't fair for him to be dirty and I was clean, because we were supposed to be doing this recovery thing together. So I decided to go get us some money and went back on the streets, looking for a trick. I remember the moment I took off my head wrap; I didn't even realize I had it on. It was a symbol of spirituality, and even if I didn't believe it, certainly tricks did, because they didn't stop until I took it off. No power.

We used the rest of the night, but we got back on track with recovery the next day. I took the program and ran with it. I did a lot of speaking engagements, acting as a showpiece, but the only problem was I never knew what was going to come out of my mouth in front of the crowd or camera. One time it was a big television conference. My friend Rooster gave me a quote about recovery, and I told him I didn't know how or when, but I was going to use that. During the question and answer part of the conference, I stood up and said, "You can feed me fish for a day and I will be full for a day, but if you teach me to fish, I will be full for a lifetime." Everyone knew what the statement meant—that his program only kept us coming back for the handout. This is not recovery! Recovery is growing and moving into a new space. You need to get into the root of who you are and why addiction has a hold on you. Adults don't need pacifiers, they need deliverance!

I ended up getting a good job with Planned Parenthood through Cecil's program and my hard work and determination. I was Community Research Counselor, and my job was to do surveys on women who were at high risk for HIV, and get them into family planning and prenatal care. I did a lot of good work for these women, but my resources were limited, and I was exposing them to the very same exploitations that I had experienced with Glide. The needs of the women were more demanding than the program was designed to meet. I became overwhelmed, and relapsed again. This time I didn't go back to any support system,—because I couldn't. I was well-known as the Support System in Recovery. It was too early in my recovery. I learned later that relapse is common in recovery—until you get true deliverance.

I eventually was handed my walking papers and a large severance paycheck. This closed the chapter on my Glide and Planned Parenthood days. I was then back to addiction and old behaviors. After years of this repeated cycle, I was downtrodden, but still searching for some type of relief. I knew I hadn't found what I was looking for. When I became discouraged, I continued to get high to fill the emptiness. Then one night Jon came in and told me that he had met a pastor who had hired him to paint scriptures on his church's wall. I had heard about this bus driver pastor, who was praying for people, but I had never met him myself. One day I wanted to see what Jon was really up to, so I went down to the church, and he was there. At first, I was scared, because just shaking the pastor's hand brought a quaking in my soul. I didn't know what it was. From that day forward, I was always finding little excuses to stop by that church. Once I got there, I couldn't stay. I would put money in an envelope, give it to the usher, and run out the door. I even stopped there with tricks, and would run in and put money in. One day I tried to just run in and run out, but Pastor Lee stopped in the middle of his Bible teaching and told me, "Come here."

I was scared. I knew that man had something, but I didn't understand it. Spirit minds the things of the Spirit, but flesh recognizes flesh. I knew he wasn't in his flesh. And he wasn't a trick. So he frightened me. I went up to the altar, and he told some of the sisters to stand behind me. He began to speak *life* into me. It was as if he didn't even see all the ugly and dirty things about me. He began to prophesy on what a mighty woman in the Lord I was going to be. I was wearing a necklace made out of turkey bones my kids had made for me, and he removed them and said, "Let these bones live again." He wasn't talking about the bones; he was talking about me. When he laid his hands on me, I felt the power of God move through me, but I didn't know what it was. He didn't try to make me stay, in fact he made a comment about the guy I had waiting in the car. That let me know he was different. He loved me from his heart, and with God's kind of love. I became his daughter.

I thank God for my Shiloh family. Our church name means a "resting place." I have definitely found rest for my soul and growth for my spirit among "these strange and peculiar people." I am also thankful for Jon for bringing me through these church doors by prayer. My pastor, George Lee, has been a father to me. He once told the church I was one of his favorites. I believe this is due to the condition I was in when God saved me. Pastor Lee used to see me at all hours of the night on the streets. He would often pull his car over, greet me, ask me how I was doing, and just pray for me right there. He never judged me. He would only say jokingly, "Where you going?"

I would always say, "Home."

He would laugh, and say, "Home is the other way."

He would speak life into me. "Sister, one day you are going to be a mighty woman in the Lord."

I would say, "Right. You got ten dollars?" He would give me the ten dollars. He also gave me a scripture, "calling things that are not and they become" (Romans 4:17). Then he would leave. I never felt pressure from him to get saved, but I felt the pressure of his love. I didn't believe what he said about me, because I knew I was a crackhead and a whore. But today, I realize I am neither of those things, and I am a mighty woman in the Lord. Those were characteristic flaws, and not who I was, just what I was doing.

My Shiloh family is closer to me than my own family—except for my children. Some people might look at this as harsh, but I remember back when Jesus was teaching in parables, someone told him that his mother was outside. His reply was, "Who is my mother or my father but those who do the will of the Lord?" (Matthew 12:50, KJV). I relate this to my Shiloh family. They were there when I was unlovable, cracked out, and out of control. My first response was to run from their cleanliness. I had so much going on, and when I came into the presence of God's anointing, I just took off running out the door.

One of the elders, Elder James, ran after me, and told me not to leave without my blessing. We called Pastor Lee on the phone, and we talked. He had ministered to me on many occasions about hope, but I couldn't hear it.

This time the seed took root. I was at the end of my rope. I was carrying around a picture of me with two black eyes that I had gotten from Jon. I know now that the picture was symbolic. Pastor Lee said to me that my hope is not in man, but in Christ Jesus.

Something that simple was the beginning of new life and a new beginning.

After I hung up, I paid attention to the choir, and they seemed to be singing songs I had been singing to myself for the last two days. As the singing went forth, I could feel something happening to me. There was a transformation occurring. I stood up and began to raise my hands, and I was saturated with love. I felt that God cared for me and heard my cries. I asked God to show me who He was. I felt free.

I stayed with Jon for another five years. I felt even more determined to make our relationship work at all costs. We went to counseling with Pastor Lee, who did not give his opinion; he gave us the Word. I remember him telling Jon, "Son, God gave you two women in one, the old and the new ..." I was the one keeping myself in bondage to him. It was evident that Jon did not want the second woman, nor the first either. He just wanted to be free, but he didn't have the guts to say it.

We didn't get high together much any more. He was with other women, though we were still living together, and I was still getting paid from my tricks. Slowly, however, we were changing. Jon did receive a blessing in church. Pastor Lee and the church prayed for him, and he was healed of a cancerous tumor in his chest.

After being prayed for by the church, my life went haywire. Just getting high to cover my emptiness wasn't working. I asked God if He was God, to show me Himself and pull me out. One day a regular trick came by, and we went into my back room to do what we always did. Something was different, though the setting was exactly the same. With my natural eye, I could only see the trick and me in that room. But there was this illuminating light and presence all over me. I told the guy that I couldn't do this any more,

"Take your dope and your money and don't ever come here again."
That was the last time I ever turned a trick.

I was feeling down because Jon and I weren't working out. This
was nothing new. Our marriage had been over for a long time. It
was just a formality, but I thought it would be a sin to divorce my
husband. It weighed heavily on my spirit, and I was looking for
an answer. Saints who are new in Christ often try to interpret the
Word on their own. This brings about confusion.

Backsliding and relapse are the same. It can last from one hour
to a lifetime. It's not just about using drugs, it's about the thoughts
and feelings, which you believe, have the power to make you fall.
This is where I first experienced relapse in drugs since I had met
Jesus. The emptiness overtook me. I was walking down Egbert
Street going home, and suddenly, I had an overwhelming urge to
buy crack. I thought one little five-shot wouldn't hurt. I peeked
around the corner to see if anybody was watching. After all, the past
three months I was marching that neighborhood with my Bible in
my hand and my kids lined up behind me saying, "Jesus lives! Auntie
don't need nothing but Jesus! He's my rock, the rock of salvation." I
didn't want to be a hypocrite, but the addict was taking over. I was
scared, but I couldn't stop myself. After the rock was placed in my
hand, I had a knot in my stomach and I had to go to the bathroom.
I thought I wasn't going to make it home. In fact I didn't.

I never gave thought to what I was going to use as a pipe. But
guess what? When I finally made it home, Jon was there. I told him
I knew he had a pipe, and to give it to me. He didn't stop me, he
just gave me the pipe. I took almost the whole rock and put it on
the pipe. I looked at Jon and told him I didn't want to corrupt him,
so I wasn't going to give him any. As I lit it, I inhaled. I felt a rush
from lightness back into the dark. I began to weep.

I heard the voice of God speak to me. It was so gentle and

so loving. He said, "What are We doing? You better get to choir rehearsal." I dropped the pipe. I was moving so quickly I can't even remember how I got to church. I rushed to the altar in a desperate need, and I told God that I was sorry. I asked Him to forgive me. I told Him that I'd betrayed Him, and would He please come back into my life and give me a new beginning. I felt the Spirit fall on me, and I hit the floor. I could hear people talking around me, but I couldn't move. I could feel myself being cleansed. It was like the dark clouds over my eyes rolled back, and I could see God the Father sitting on the throne. His eyes seemed blue, but it doesn't represent a race, but—representing his extended invitation. I could see spiritually the glory of God in scenery that I've never seen on earth before. I could see the beginning of time, and it enhanced my belief about the ending of time.

This was the last time that I ever used crack cocaine.

I asked God to let me be sensitive to the smell so that it would smell horrible and offensive. I also wanted to recognize that cocaine spirit on other addicts for two reasons: I could pray for them with compassion and not judgment, and I would be grateful whenever I smelled that powerful foul smell. It would always remind me of where God brought me from and never to go back down that road again. Thank you, Lord!

Family is not always the best source for recovery. Usually as an addict you have burned them all out, and even though they love you, it's hard for them to trust or believe that the old dope fiend in you has changed.

I had to be careful around my family in my recovery. Once I met Jesus, the church people became my family, so I had to quit beating myself up trying to make my natural family believe I had changed. When you follow Jesus, change is in your talk, your walk, and your way. You don't have to prove anything to anybody. Just follow Jesus.

I made my amends by apologizing to Jesus for my behavior. As far as my family is concerned, I have apologized for things I said or did, but I don't allow them to beat me down with my past.

The Bible says that once you have said what you need to say, if it's not received, you knock the dust off your feet and keep stepping (Matthew 10:14). This tool is not an easy tool to use, but practice makes perfect. I know I had wronged my children, my mothers, and many others, but the best amends that I can make, or have already made, is the person that I am today, God's virtuous woman.

I had a special friend, Alley Boy from the streets, who died in 2000. When I told him about giving my life to Jesus, he said, "Jerus! You can try this Jesus thing for a year. If it doesn't work, you can always go back to the streets!" Then we laughed. Later I knew that was drug talk, always wanting a way out. Thank you, God, for using Alley Boy as a messenger to bring about change in my life.

If you are the saved family member, you can be an inspiration. Perhaps your testimony can help another family member. I got the opportunity to experience this with my Auntie Cedra's daughter, Tessa. Her children are like my nieces, even though they are my first cousins. I can remember spending a lot of time with Auntie Cedra's children, but Tessa seemed to pattern herself after me. It's a scary thing when somebody idolizes you, and you're living a lie. Being a person who's filled with compassion, I totally missed it. I saw signs of her addictive behavior when she grew up. Unfortunately, at that time I couldn't help her because I was doing the same thing.

When Jesus came into my life, He reorganized it so Tessa was able to see me in a different light. People may think that saints of God are not supposed to endure hardships—that's a lie! In my early recovery, the electricity went off; the bill was over fifteen hundred dollars. I didn't know how I was going to pay it. The church took an offering for me; Marie gave me five hundred dollars, and all together, I had about eight hundred dollars for the bill.

They simply refused to negotiate with me at all. I decided to stop stressing about it, I bought some candles, and a neighbor named Stevenson offered to run a long electrical cord from his house to mine. This was acceptable. All I cared about at the time was being saved and staying clean. It might have been a horrible time in society's eyes, living with children and no utilities, but God knows what He is doing. We were having the time of our lives—mama was off of crack cocaine and staying home!

One evening Tessa came by the house, and she needed a place to stay. I explained the circumstances but told her she was welcome to stay. Her spirit seemed to be broken, but I didn't pressure her. I just loved her. I told her that God loved her, that He sees her turmoil. She just needed to trust and believe Him. I didn't know then that she had entered into that whole drug scene, but God had her with us for a reason. My children and I went on with our lives, going to church, praying in the house, and we invited her to prayer. She soon confided in me that she used to go to the Church of Redeem in Sunnydale by the Cow Palace, a sister-church that my church shared space with in the early days. I didn't know that about her. She said she had been touched by God before, but she was a backslider. I began to witness to her, and soon she wanted to go to church with me. She was faithful. It was her birthday, and instead of going out and partying like most folks, including me, would do, we went to clean the house of the Lord—clean! We scrubbed the pulpit, washed the walls, vacuumed, and had the place shining.

She said she was ready to see her pastor, Lavonne Bell. They were having a revival. We arrived early, which wasn't unusual for me. Since God had touched my life, I was always arriving places early.

The Spirit of God just poured into that service. We were shouting and jumping up and down; people were falling out all over the place, and it was real. Tessa just totally surrendered herself that night. She lay on the floor for forty-five minutes, screaming out to Jesus. When we returned home, singing and praising God as we walked along, although our house was dark, the place was lit up. The presence of God was lighting up the whole house. God started a good work in Tessa. Even though this was not the end of her addiction, a seed was planted. She soon left me and went back out. Today she has a husband that she asked God for, and three daughters and a son. I continued to pray and wait for her day of deliverance, because I knew it was at hand, and now it has come to pass.

Meanwhile, my biological mother Brenda moved to California to live with me. Jon was in jail at the time. Andy and I decided we wanted to get married. I was lonely, and although I had been living with Jon and married to him for ten years, the last five we had no intimacy. I wanted a husband, and I wanted to marry someone I knew and who really knew me. Andy and I had grown closer through the years, and he inspired me to move on. He gave me the courage to finally get a divorce from Jon. Brenda offered to pay for it. Andy and I went to visit Jon in jail, and Andy told him. I was silent. Jon showed no emotion, even though I knew he cared. Andy was also sleeping with an old girlfriend who I had to tell about our marriage. She was angry, and never forgave me. By the end of a week, Andy had pulled one of his famous numbers. He had run off with my new car my mom just bought me, and all of her Avon products in the trunk. I believe this was his way of letting himself off the hook, and me too. The marriage was a fantasy, but his betrayal broke up our friendship. He sold the products and smoked up all the Avon money, but after a week, he returned the car and apologized. We both knew that he was not right for me. Some years later, I forgave him. When we see each other, I still have love for him—he is still my "brother." We're still known as brother and sister.

AND THE BEAT GOES ON

Many people have different characters inside; I just happen to live through all of mine. They have different names and personalities. There's La Wanda, the compulsive, no nonsense business woman. She authorizes all aspects of the gifts God has given her. She's the writer, the control freak—she gets things done! Then there's Chickie, the hustler, hooker, and street girl. Her skills promote the business. However, she needs a tight rein due to her spontaneous nature, which has gotten her into trouble over the years. Perhaps she's the reason that my children all have different last names. *If it felt good, do it!* If the one you were with wouldn't do it, have somebody else do it. And make them pay to do it. If you want no strings attached, pay them to do it for you.

Next is Miss Cap. (I was called that because my boyfriend at the time, Lou, had the street name of Redcap.). She likes to take risks, even to the extent that it landed her in jail. She was the character that sold cocaine, daring to enter a dangerous male dominated world. The truth of it is that I knew I was beautiful, talented, intelligent, and I could keep the attentions of men. I was Redcap's showpiece, until all his training taught me the business, and I became a better dope dealer than he was.

Then came Ja Rasta. She was that whole Rastafaric Muslim Wrap Wearing Sistergirl, stuck in all her Darkness. At that time, it was "culturally correct" to be all those things (if you are confused).

I was confused! I had Buddhist, Muslim, Nam Renge Kyo ("Yo Reggae Quo"), and Jesus operating at the same time. Whatever got me through the door was it—for the moment!

I walked around doing things but not believing that anyone could see me. It was as if I was a shadow. When I lived in darkness, I had blinders on my eyes, and couldn't see what was right in front of me. I was too caught up getting high, and any time any light would be shed on my way of living, somehow the drug cast a shadow I couldn't see past.

Today, meet Jerus. I acquired this name while lying on a jailhouse floor, because all eight beds were full. I was sick with a temperature of 102 degrees, calling out to the guards for some medical attention. However, there was no medical attention for me. I was enraged and screamed, "I've got rights!" Soon, I learned that I had given up all my rights the day I sold my first package of cocaine. Then some of the women started taking care of me, and gave me some of their antibiotics and pain medicine.

I lay there on the floor and went into a spiritual realm. I believe that this was my first time as an adult having true fellowship with God. I can't say I really heard His voice at this time, but it was as if a Word was put inside of me while I lay there drifting. The Word was: "From this day forward, you will be known as Jerus, which stands for Jerusalem, new nation." The seed was planted but wouldn't come to flower for many years. I left that jail telling people that my name was now Jerus.

It didn't take long until many people—even friends and family— were calling me that. Years later, after being filled with the Holy Ghost, I have an understanding of what "new nation" means. It meant through God changing my life that the lives of my children, grandchildren, and their children—and possibly other children— would be changed through salvation.

This is where recovery comes in. Being a seasoned Christian now, I am aware that the more victorious I am, the more attacks I have in my family, my finances, my joy, my peace, and my recovery. But I thank God that He has installed His Word in my heart. It's become my Etch-a-Sketch. I have to constantly speak life into myself, quoting God's scriptures. It's a spiritual battle, and sometimes I feel I'm fighting it all alone, but the more I use God's words as a tool, the more I can stand up for myself and fight. I've learned to understand that my happiness and true joy are not about "people, places, and things." Life is filled with good, bad, suffering, obstacles, and doubt, but my joy or my peace has nothing to do with those things.

My true joy and peace is in Christ Jesus. I have to go back to my beginnings and the mire and muck that He first brought me out of, and then all of the circumstances that I'm going through now mean absolutely nothing. It's only another trial. And I know that after this one passes, another will be coming. Therefore, my peace returns quickly. That is the basis of my recovery, getting clean and staying clean. Many times in my walk with Christ, the Word has been bitter bread, but I trusted God and swallowed, and I have been blessed in doing so.

HERE COMES THE GREAT FALL

I married a man from a different culture. Puerto Rican men, like many from island cultures, seem to me to be self-centered, taking women for granted as well as the sanctimony of marriage. I didn't understand the culture or the language, and this became a problem for me. I was willing to marry him on blind faith. I know God told me to marry Vince, but I must admit I was already involved with him. Vince was a good guy, for the most part. I see how I was the problem. I was attracted to him for many years, but I crossed the line—I was saved, and he wasn't. I had a twenty-year crush on this man, and to me that was a lifetime. He was like fine wine. I had forsaken the Lord to have him. Yes, I stole him, by sleeping with him before I married him. Many times, I would cry after being with him because I knew it was wrong. He would say to me, "Don't cry. I'm going to marry you."

The desires of your heart and the lust of your flesh both will cost you something. However, do you want to pay the price? I know that the word says, "It is better to marry than to burn." (1 Corinthians 7:9). So we did.

Before we married, I asked Vince what he wanted of me. He replied, "Don't ever change." That should have been a warning sign, but I didn't see it. I was in love. I've always tried to practice agape love, to maintain discipline, loving action, and humility, no matter who was right. However, my husband failed to tell me that his love would be conditional. He had the ability to be cruel and to punish, and to withhold sex as a tool of power. *Or so he thought.* What he didn't realize was that I've been a sinner all my life, and the only reason that I haven't been touched by another man during our marriage is God's grace.

Money was the weakest link between Vince and me. He wants it; I want it, but the only thing holding both of us back from having it is each other. Too much emphasis has been placed on the value of a dollar. It was my belief that the value of our marriage was in our being together. Most marriages are way too fragile today. People can experience life and death and stay together, but a checkbook can tear a couple apart. We often forget all the sacrifices we were willing to make in the beginning, but somewhere along the line the sin of familiarity sets in, and we take each other for granted. Our vision becomes distorted and narrow. We look with envy at other's lives, wishing and imitating. But when the picture becomes clear, it was their life, not ours.

Years ago, I had visions, dreams, and nightmares about my husband and vulgar party scenes. I kept trying to reach him and pull him out, but he was mocking me. I would wake up drenched in sweat, screaming, "Papi!" He would comfort me in my distress and tell me everything was all right, but even then, I knew something was wrong, and hadn't been right for a long time.

SUITOR'S CHECKLIST

I always hear people say, "Follow your heart." That is the worst advice to ever give anyone. The heart can be wicked, cunning, and often is led by the desires of your flesh. The statement should be, "Follow the One that lives in your heart." I know that you can't focus on externals, but you need to do a checklist. Remember about *rules*—they apply in every part of your life. Use them!

Believe me, I am down with romance, marriage, love, and all that, but there is something more that is needed for a lasting marriage. There is an order to the universe, as Marie says. We women are out of order, because we have switched roles. God has set high standards for us. It shows in the way He loves us unconditionally, takes care of us, forgives us, protects us, and provides for us. He is the Head of our lives. When we get married, our husband becomes the head of our house, but God is the Head of both our lives. Our husbands take on the responsibility as our protector, provider, and all the rest.

Here is where the checklist comes in. If a man asks you to marry him, can he fulfill the basic obligations of a husband? Is he a man of God? Does he tithe? Does he have a job? We know not all men have jobs. If not, tell him to come back courting when he does. Is he generous with more than just his sperm? How many baby-mamas does he have? And how many babies? This will give you an indication of how faithful or unfaithful he will be. Is he supporting his children? Ask yourself if you are willing to raise his other children. If not, *warning! Red Flags!* Do not approach Go. Flee!

Other important considerations are his finances, his family background, and how he copes with good and bad situations. Does he have a history of violence? A criminal history? Or is he on drugs? Or is he bisexual? These things are predictors of what's to come, and it ain't pretty. You will catch hell, unless he has been reborn. No woman can change a man before or after marriage. Your love, your sex, and your babies will not change his character or his habits. This is something only God can do. Before you marry, let God finish His job. In the end, you will know if this man should be your husband. God will show you everything. We choose to ignore the warning signs, because we don't want to be alone. Or we think our love will overcome all obstacles. Sooner or later, the very warning signs you ignored surface, and the truth is out. You knew it but didn't want to see it. Then you're stuck!

That night it was quiet in our house. I had done all the shopping for the baskets, and my husband still wasn't home. In fact, this was day five that he hadn't come home. He had text messaged me two days ago saying he was in Napa working (at his limo job), and he couldn't call, but he would be home. Lately, he had not been answering my phone calls and had been very impatient, hard, and distant. After my accident and injury with Muni, I was disabled for two years, so we were struggling financially. For the past six years, my life has revolved around the church, myself, my children, and now my grandchildren.

This year was an unusual Thanksgiving for me, even more interesting than the last. Last year I spent two days cooking and preparing a wonderful feast. Unfortunately, this was the beginning of trouble in my marriage, where I saw the first warning signs of Vince's adultery. He came home early Thanksgiving morning, and we argued about a woman's phone number and text messages on his cell phone. It was evident to me that something was going on. Although, I wanted to believe what he was saying was true, in my heart I knew he was lying. I thought maybe he was coming home to get his things and leave, but instead he went to bed. The house was quiet. I was tired after all the cooking, emotional weeping, cursing, and threatening to kill him, which I had done throughout the night. The kids all had gone somewhere else, and I just served him his meal in silence. I was afraid if I said something, I would become very dangerous. After he awoke, he ate my cooking and continued to claim that nothing was happening. I continued to "be his wife" and act like I believed him.

JESUS CHRIST IS LORD

For many years, I was confused. It seemed to me that Marie had always been surrounded by false gods, from Buddhas to angels. Sherrie and I went to Marie's house to braid her hair, and I had an overwhelming urge to address Marie about her statues. From my studies in the Bible, it speaks on idols and false gods (Leviticus 19:4). I resented all the different churches and practices like séances, psychics, Ouija boards, and new age churches that Marie had exposed me to. It was too many forms of religions, and I couldn't grasp onto any of them. I knew there was a God, but which one was real? Marie was downstairs. My heart was beating fast as I looked around her living room. When she came upstairs, she was very apologetic for a mix-up about her hair, which did not need braiding. All that did not matter—now. My mouth was open, but the words wouldn't fall out. All I could hear was "Honor thy Father and thy mother" (Exodus 20:12). With my backwards thinking, I thought it meant, "Don't speak." Deep inside of me, I could feel the pressure of God wanting me to speak. What I did was to tell Marie, "I hope you're not going to be mad at me, but what is it with all these statues? What do they mean?"

Marie said, "Why do you think I'm going to get mad, La Wanda?" She never fails to pull her MSW-mommy thing. Sometimes this threw me off. But it didn't throw God off. He wanted me to leave there with some new revelation that day.

At first, she did seem to be a little annoyed, but that happens in families. When the Spirit of God is moving, things fall into place, even though its seems that they are out of place.

Marie said, "That statue over there reminds me of the heavy load that that man carries. It enables me to carry my heavy load, to know that I can do it."

I thought that was Jesus' job, my mind whispered to me.

I said, "The reason that I am questioning this is because of your relationship with Allen and this 'monument to the spirit' that the two of you said you were going to build. What kind of monument to what spirit?"

There are many spirits, I thought. *Which one is operating here?*

Then she said, "I was paying him to do God's vision in our landscape remodeling, and he wouldn't follow the blue print. I felt betrayed, and I don't deal with non-truth."

The spirit that Marie was speaking through scared me because I felt the same way about my business. For the first time, I was really starting to notice how much I was like her in many ways.

After we cooled down, we went into the dining room and sat at the table. I was feeling pretty good that she and I weren't going to fall out about the statues, at least not today. Confronting Marie is a big job that takes courage, but I had done it.

After every accomplishment—look out, here comes a trial! I began to talk to Marie about my marriage and upcoming anniversary. This was year six of my marriage to Vince. In my wedding book, it says that iron and candy are the anniversary gifts. I didn't know what this meant. I told Marie that I thought I was the candy, and perhaps the iron meant that somehow, I'm supposed to be cold and hard, but that's not me. *Whenever I look at my husband, I want to kiss and hug him. Now I've got to slap him too?*

She looked at me with her loving mommy eyes and shook her head. She said, "La Wanda, you are backwards! Iron means to be strong!"

DEEP IN THE VALLEY

If it wasn't for this ache in the bottom of my stomach, I would think I am dead. Way down deep where my soul lives, this is where all my gray areas are stored. I know that nothing good lives in that part of me, because when I dwell there it brings about depression, reminders of rejection, and utter confusion. My life is filled with signs and wonders of God. I only need to look, listen, and pay attention. I have this way of asking God for a closer walk, but to whom much is given, much is required (1 Corinthians 4:2). I know that in my spirit and in my heart is where Jesus lives.

I went to church last Sunday. Pastor Lee had not returned since the death of his wife. I heard that he preached at a homegoing so I knew he'd be back soon. It seems at times like these I could use him to talk to, but I wouldn't dare lay my problems on him when he is the one in need. We have some solid elders and ministers standing in for him. I went to church for choir rehearsal. I was so downtrodden that it showed, and I didn't try to cover it up. God is too real for me to try to be fake. Ironically, this was a Friday, and I always remember getting saved on a Friday night, and getting filled with the Holy Spirit on a Wednesday. It's almost like twelve years later and I'm at the same point in my life, but this time I'm saved.

Elder Bailey said he had a word for me from the Lord. I really didn't want to receive any words, but when you belong to God you have to eat the bitter root to get to the sweet nectar. One has to stay humble and have a teachable spirit to serve the Lord, even when you don't want to. I made sure to go get the word from him. The elder didn't know my circumstances, but he began to speak things only God knew. He said, "God is going to reveal all to you, and then you will understand." After he gave me that word, I could appreciate the power of God that dwells in him.

Three months ago, Marie gave me the meaning of iron, which means to be strong. The next day, the first shoe dropped. I packed Vince's suitcase and asked him to leave though, actually, he had already left months before.

After receiving the word that Sunday, the second shoe dropped. I was busy preparing for my spa day gala event. I was excited and focused. The phone rang, and a strange woman began to ask me about my relationship with my husband. I asked her who she was, but she refused to tell me her name. However, she let me know that she had been sleeping with him for the past two years, and she had just found out he was married. She went on to say he said he wasn't happy, then she let me know that he was now living in San Francisco with yet another woman and her children. Actually, I didn't know about her, but I knew that he was tipping with someone. I asked her if she was angry because he was cheating on her. Hadn't she noticed the rings on his fingers? She tried to be coy by saying, "He said he got them from his broads."

I said, "Yes, but this broad's name is 'wife,' and I've already had the best of him." Then I hung up. She shook my core. I was pacing the floor trying to shake it, but actually inside I already knew the truth. I just wanted him to come and tell me himself. Many times, I have opened the door to honest conversation with him, but he continued to lie. Pastor always told me that my husband was a gift from God. He helped me raise my children who were not his own. He never behaved inappropriately with them. He became their loving and protective father, and then grandfather. He was a gift for that season in my life. He was good for the girls—however, he didn't teach my son to stand as a man through difficult times—he taught him to run.

FINDING MYSELF

Sometimes you can underestimate what God can do. The very thing you think you're incapable of doing becomes what you must do. For instance, baking is something I thought I couldn't do successfully, but I found out that not only could I do it, I could do it very well, and make money with it. Recently my business partners and I were forced to opened a little business called "I Gotta Need," a unique gift baskets enterprise. We were all struggling financially, and so we resorted to the gifts that God has given women through the ages— baking and cooking—in order to get the capital we needed for the real business, personalized baskets. I realized that now that I'm really serious and committed to starting my own business, obstacles keep appearing in my path. I have constant pain in one area of my body or another, and the fear of failure haunts me and taunts me.

I was doing errands, and I thought I had everything all set up and ready to go, but I found myself lost. I knew I was going to Abby's house for business, but I couldn't seem to get there. I kept taking wrong turns, getting on the wrong freeway, and taking the wrong exits. I ended up in the Posey Tunnel to Alameda, and lost another fifteen minutes before I got back to Oakland. When I get lost, I seem to experience a character change. Fear comes to me in the form of doubts, disbelief, loss of self, and something tells me I'm not going to make it. I feel this is directly connected to the gray areas in my life. I become that little girl again who had no control over what happened to her. Now as an adult, whenever I feel like I'm succeeding and using all the gifts I've been blessed with, that little girl comes back. This is the grip that failure has on me. My eyes begin to water, and I just start weeping. Then I have to rely on God to get me back, that is, I have to start speaking the Word of God to myself. As I speak it, it begins to take on life in me, and it's my entrance back into peace.

By the time I got to my destination that day, La Wanda had returned. When I saw my friend still in her nightclothes at noon, I was hard on her, because we were operating a business. She had no idea of what state I was in just fifteen minutes ago. After I go through one of my dark moments, I become very focused and productive.

It reassured me that my life in Christ was different, and so was my marriage. I really don't know what happened between my friend Abby and me. She had told me she and her aunt were feuding again. Then I heard nothing. After five days of no communication from her, I wanted to stop the silence. I needed answers. I tried numerous times to call her and go by her house to see her, but there was no answer. She was avoiding me—and my daughter Sharon. Nothing we tried brought any answers.

However, I was a very determined person. I decided one day to drive by her house. She was sitting on her porch. I turned the corner and parked. I looked up, and she had gone into the house. I could not believe that she did not want to face me. She had learned so much about me, and I was shocked that she refused to communicate about what was going on.

I drove around the block, and she had come back out on the porch and sat down. I stopped my car in the middle of the street and looked at her with confusion. She struggled to wave. I pulled into her driveway and asked her what was going on. She began to complain about her problems, and I shared with her about Vince and me. I explained to her that business must go on. Then she said that she would call me and explain. She never did. I got a call from another friend telling me Abby was sick so I jumped in my car and went to see her. We got a chance to clear the air and find friendship again, forgiving one another. I would go and see her. We never had differences again, and every time I left, I would hug her like it would be my last time seeing her. Later Vince told me that she probably pushed me away because she had actually just learned she was dying. I hadn't realized that, but it made sense.

Later on that night, I was sitting alone in the living room working on personalizing the baskets. It was silent, a moment I got to spend with myself. Sometimes I am scared of those moments, because I don't know what I'm going to learn about me. I had gone from brain surgery to addiction, a seventeen-year journey during which I lived spontaneously, always caught up in the moment, not giving thought to the past or the future.

What am I afraid of? Even though there is peace, I know that the fear is always present too. In that quiet moment, I wanted to see what I was afraid of. I made a decision to trust that God within would be there with me. How He revealed His Presence was through my hands touching the baskets. As I worked on the baskets, I could feel that the spirit of God's touch was there in the arts and crafts. I saw the beauty in what I was doing, and I remembered I had forgotten that I could create things of beauty with my hands. It is my gift. This realization brought me so much joy that I can open up and discover all the things about me that are good, productive, and nurturing.

I continued to make the same mistakes over and over again. I was listening, but I wasn't allowing the Word to penetrate me so I could use it as a tool. It was like water falling on shallow ground.

The rain was coming down hard as I drove to say goodbye to my friend Abby, who went on to be with the Lord. As I entered the mortuary doors, I could feel fear coming upon me. I haven't had a lot of experience with death, but this is the year to experience and learn about all things pertaining to life. It was a long walk down the hall. I told myself I wasn't going to look for any fault, but just say goodbye. I approached her body, not knowing what to expect. She was dark. There was no light. It was just an empty shell laying there. I didn't even recognize her. She was dressed in a pink suit, and her dreads were covered with a head scarf tied in a bow. It was as if someone who didn't really know her prepared her to meet the King. She should have been dressed in gold; she wore that a lot.

Even though I was starting to feel agitated, I reminded myself that I wasn't going to look for faults. I talked to her as if she were with me. I thanked her for our time together, and for being my friend. I let her know I was so glad we had a chance to make up. I told her that she gave me the gift of understanding how to really forgive, forgive myself and accept forgiveness. I know she wouldn't have liked the sad songs, but I had to sing a verse of "Precious Lord." I sang it with all my heart and felt I had kissed her in the Spirit. I told her I would be joining her one day. As I was leaving, I felt a strength and understanding.

Death frightens me, but I'm learning that it must come to everyone. When families are grieving, having to deal with finances brings out the true nature of the beast, especially when there's no money for the burial. We need to live with and leave with our business in order.

Seeing Abby today has reminded me that keeping focused on the Lord is definitely what I need in my life. Pastor Lee told me that when you have made up your mind not to go back, that's when all hell breaks loose. Trials and tribulations that I'm having to face are meant to do evil, but the Lord stands there and He turns the situation around. Although at times I might waver, I know that He is going to bring me out, and that my end is victorious.

I was hired at San Francisco's Vital Records Department as a Health

Worker 1, and I decided I wanted to see my deceased son's records. It was the first time I ever had the courage to even consider looking at those records. I pulled his death certificate first, and then his birth certificate. I held them in my hands and felt like I was finally ready to deal with these memories. I see now that was my first step in accepting death as a healing process in a positive sense.

Raising children is the hardest job anyone could ever have. There are many guidebooks, and there are many authors, but each child is different. You have to practically rewrite the book with every child. The life of the parent is also the life of the child, but only for a season. Once they have reached adulthood, they have the choice of becoming whomever they choose to be. In some instances, children take a lifetime to discover their separateness from their parents. Parents change as time goes on, some for the worse, some for the better, but our children reflect who we are at any given time. There are visible signs of how you are parenting: when you do a really good job, only a few people recognize it, but when you make mistakes, everybody notices your weaknesses in your children's behavior and you—especially in my circumstances.

My oldest daughter, Kara, was a precious gem, although through my addiction she was probably hit the hardest. She watched me go through many years of drug use and street life. I love her for her continuous courage, strength, and belief in me. We used to go everywhere together. I had a problem leaving her with anybody. If I went to a club, she went to the club. We were joined together. I used to sing to her, rock her in the rocking chair, and brush her hair.

However, as the tables turned, my addiction took over my life. My parenting skills diminished. In the beginning, I was always an organized mother, with scheduled times for scheduled events. Something as simple as bathing my child every day at noon, being postponed to six, or *I'll do it tomorrow*. Soon the drugs were taking over and stability in Kara's life was falling apart. I couldn't explain it nor control it. I didn't even notice it at the time. As a young child, she adapted to whatever my lifestyle was. It was no picnic for her. She was put in foster care, not once but twice, and she also lived with my Auntie Cedra.

At one time she was even put in Saint Mary's Hospital in the pediatric psych ward. Kara was rebelling against our separation. She knew her mom had problems, but she would rather be with me than without me. She recognized how to play the social service system to her advantage at a young age. She and I had supervised visits where we were monitored. Kids know about drugs. There were times when I would come late because I had been up all night getting high. Whenever I came through the doors to greet her, she would reach for me and hug me, showing me unconditional love. I felt bad because I really did want her with me, but I couldn't let go of the drugs, yet. I always arrived with a picnic lunch and gifts for her. She was ecstatic, and we would have a good time. That's the mother that she remembers. But at the end of the visit, I would see her little face fill with such sadness, but she would rarely cry. She acted like "a big girl," and I would promise that one day I would come to get her. I would leave, and though I felt good about the visit, I felt terrible that I was putting her through such hell.

One time when she was about eight, she had an incident in foster care. I was told that she threatened to kill herself. They took her to the hospital, and she was admitted. They allowed me to come and see her. When I looked at her, she was heavily medicated, sitting in a chair, almost lifeless. I asked what was wrong with her, and why was she so drowsy and unresponsive. They explained to me that they wanted to keep her subdued for her own safety. I became outraged. I didn't believe that was the way to deal with her behavior was to medicate her so heavily. I also believed they were not willing to deal with her emotional problems.

After I called Marie and she came to visit, the medications were reduced. Kara was then able to enjoy our visits. While she was there, I could visit her all day any day with no restrictions. By being in the hospital, she had figured out a way for us to see each other every day—and we did. After a few months in the hospital, Kara was released to a Christian foster family in Santa Rosa.

The couple were good to Kara and me, even though they had three of their own children and had taken in four or five other children with problems. It was their goal to reunite us. They invited me to come to dinner on many occasions, and supported my efforts at recovery. I was going to parenting meetings and leading an active role in recovery for myself and other addicts. However, Kara's social worker Mary was old and bitter, and did not believe in the possibility of change. We got into horrible arguments regarding what was best for Kara. I was resenting and resisting her authority over my daughter. Circumstances didn't change until I stopped fighting her, and began to work on my self-righteous attitude. This woman was in my life because of my mistakes, and I was the one with the problem. Drugs still had a grip on me, even though I was clean.

GIVE THANKS

I had no intentions of cooking for Thanksgiving. I'd somehow lost the desire to cook at that moment in my life. When Vince stopped eating my cooking, it had an effect on me. My desire to express my love through cooking was wounded. My kids and I were supposed to have dinner in two places this year, at (my daughter) Jerri's boyfriend's mom's (Dreese's) house, and at my sister-cousin Lola's house. Dreese was supposed to cook all the food. My job was to provide basket gifts.

I got a phone call that Dreese needed to use my oven to cook one of the turkeys. Of course, I said yes, but yes to using my oven, not to my cooking the turkey. So they shouldn't have been mad when it burned. I was busy sulking in my room. I said I was in no shape for cooking! The outside was blackened—in some cultures, they like it like that. The dog enjoyed it very much, and we enjoyed Dreese's other turkey.

I definitely did not want to miss getting to Lola's house. I needed to talk to family members about the book, and no one was returning my calls. However, I knew where to find them on Thanksgiving day. To my surprise, I found out more about myself as a teenager. At first I didn't want to believe that I did so much sneaky stuff. Lola said not only did I do it, I blamed it on her, and that's why she used to kick my Jordache. I had blanked out my skills and techniques with locks, but as soon as she said I used to pick the locks to get into rooms to get money, and then lock it back up, I knew she was telling the truth! So, I am admitting my shady behavior and asking for everyone to forgive the thief in me.

Recently my husband and I had filed for bankruptcy, which freaked us out, but to me it symbolized a new beginning. Most of the kids are gone, there are no more bill collectors calling, and I have been able to open a new business. Life is better for me! On the other hand, my husband is still doing the same job for the same reasons, and is stuck in the past. He lacks vision, seeing only what is before his eyes. The grass is always greener somewhere else. He sees all the problems as my fault. I knew he was hurting, but so was I. He refused to open up and share his feelings with me, or to allow us to work through our problems together. He threw me to the wolves.

As I sat in the living room alone, I was restless and grief stricken. I was thinking all kinds of ugly thoughts about him cheating, lying, and letting me down. To be honest, I felt rejected. I began to talk to Jesus, saying, "Lord, I always get to this fork in the road where nobody wants to go the whole distance with me. What's wrong with me? Why do I continue to get rejected?"

God's response was to put me to work on my baskets, and before I knew it, it was four o'clock Monday morning. I had done twenty-four Easter baskets and ten caregiver baskets, all filled and decorated, and I still had time on my hands. I lay in bed, but I just couldn't sleep. All of a sudden, I jumped out of bed, opened up Vince's suitcase, and started shoving all his stuff in there. I then called him on his cell phone. Of course, he didn't answer, so I pulled the old trick women have done for years, I left a message. The message was: "I'll drop your stuff off at your job on my way to work." Five minutes later the phone rang. He said, "You don't have to drop it off at my job! I'll come and get it tonight."

"Fine," I said. I got myself together and went to work. In fact I made it there every day for two weeks, and that doesn't usually happen, because of my disability and depression. That workday was the longest day of my life, so it seemed, as I waited to go home and see if he picked up his stuff while I was gone. I entered the house with my heart pounding. All I could hear was the scripture, "A foolish woman tears up her own house." (Proverbs 14:1, KJV) I was thinking, "If I don't do this, my house is already torn down!" I unlocked the door to my room. His suitcase was still sitting there. I took a deep breath. I tried to wait up for him, but I was tired from the night before and finally went to bed. Around 11:30 p.m. he came in, looking all worn and torn. He was operating in a defensive spirit, but God is not controlled by that. I told him I wanted to deal in truth.

"Tell me what is going on," I said.

"I am tired of this environment. I'm stuck in the past and I keep talking about it."

I asked him, "Are you talking to anybody about our problems?"

"Anybody that'll listen," he said, with his Puerto Rican drawl.

Except me, I thought to myself. I replied, "You are bad mouthing me with people? Baby, you're supposed to protect and provide for me, not take my covering off!"

He was quiet. I asked him if we were through, or were we getting "space." He said that he needed time. I told him we needed to take care of things. He said he would help me with the bills and not leave me stranded. This was the first break up or separation from a man that actually was intimate. We were talking and not fighting. There are two ways of looking at this situation: the way the world looks at it (which is the eyes of flesh), and the way the Spirit looks at it. Either I could destroy my marriage right now, or I could let him go and he would return if it was God's will. I tried not to cry. He came over, and he kissed and held me. He told me he loved me. Then he took his suitcase to the car and came back. He was having as much trouble leaving as I had in not telling him to stay. I wanted to jump off the bed but God wouldn't let me move. Vince reached down again to hug me, and kissed me. We held onto each other.

"Don't put nothing between us," I said softly. I put a letter that I had written him in his pocket. We call them kites, a habit we started many years ago when we were in jail. The kite was to thank him for his many years of love, affection, and devotion to the children and myself…that he had treated me with such respect and honored me as a wife, and that I could not accept anything less. I told him I loved him and my desire was for him. Then he left.

I was horrified, hurting, and feeling rejected again, when Sharon my daughter called and told me to snap out of it and go take a "Sistah-girl" bath. Against my will, I did it.

"Thank you, God, for always comforting me when I am down." Then I told Him I wanted to let go of my husband, to stop calling him and trying to force myself into his life. If he wanted me, he knew where to find me. You know, it was rough. In one week, I had lost a best friend (and business partner) and my husband.

Unscrupulous! This is the behavior that describes my in-laws. I woke up one morning taking inventory of myself and my relationship with Vince and his family, particularly remembering my trip to Puerto Rico right after we restated our wedding vows. It was a very romantic and loving atmosphere, but no sex. I was deceived. At first, I thought that I was special in the lives of Vince's mother and sister, but although that roast chicken meal they served me was truly delicious, after I learned the truth it felt like the Last Supper. It seemed to me they knew what Vince was doing outside our marriage and were keeping it secret from me, especially because I didn't speak Spanish. If I'm wrong, I apologize, but later when the truth came out, they weren't there for me. Both of these ladies have had the exact same experience of being cheated on by their great loves, but they had no compassion for me. They just seemed to accept the other woman with no regard for who I was in his life. It seemed cold as ice. Maybe it's cultural, but it isn't right. I emailed his sister reminding her of my years of devotion to Vince, and told her I felt devalued by his family when they entertained his girlfriend in their home. I also explained that a man learns values from his family, wrongs and rights. Vince's family's behavior seemed disrespectful to me. I said some rude and nasty things, and then I apologized for that.

I thanked God that I had been hurt but unscathed.

I learned something important in my credit counseling class. Men and women react differently to financial pressures. My husband was stressed *during* the process of filing bankruptcy and dealing with our debts. After it was settled, I was the one having the difficulties. A lot of it is retraining, learning to do things the right way, instead of the quick way. I misjudged my husband by not understanding what he was going through as the head of the household. Now he too had the space to forgive himself and me and begin again, if he chose.

Recently, I had a moment of clarity. It happened when I walked into the YMCA. A memory popped up about me when I left home as a teenager and was separating from Marie. My youngest daughter Deena left home at seventeen and separated herself from me. She had been weighing heavily on my mind. She was about to have a baby, and she had disconnected from me—and her family. At first, I ranted and raved because I couldn't see why she wouldn't include her family in her life. Days went by and we didn't hear a word from her. She was in a relationship that was unhealthy. There had been domestic violence, and she was shut off from her friends and a social life. I had been asking God why. *What did I do wrong? Why doesn't that kid love me?* I really saw myself as having done the same things that my daughter was doing. Like her, I wanted to have my own life and not be judged.

But guess what? At that moment I realized, your life is not your own in a family. A family bears the burden of good, bad, and indifferent for every member. I can see now that the choices I made and how I carried them out hurt both Marie and my family. Suddenly, I really wished that Marie had not stopped calling and invading my life. I needed her more than I was willing to admit. One of the most important lessons I learned from this was not to let go spiritually, no matter what. I knew I had to give Deena her space but keep reaching for her, leaving the door open but not lecturing, just trusting that she would know right from wrong. The Lord will always reveal it. She will come to it in her own time, just as I did. For the first time when I was lecturing her, she said, "Mom, please don't do that." And I heard her, and I apologized. I don't know when her transformation will come, but my job is to love her, pray for her, and to be a grandmother to my grandson.

History tends to repeat itself. The theme of separation and rejection began with my own mother Brenda. She never was allowed to raise me. I think it was because she was very young, maybe fifteen, and she was even younger in mind. Not only did she become pregnant because of being raped, she was the victim of her mother's sister's aunt's husband. He was supposed to take her to pick up dinner rolls, and instead, he assaulted her.

Recently she told me that she told God that she was going to "give this baby back to Him," meaning that this baby (me) was going to be not a burden but a blessing. She was feeling really down when she told me that. I didn't know how to react, but I did tell her that through me, she is blessed with many grandchildren and God is in my life! I feel sorry for my mom sometimes. She's had a rough life, with many broken relationships and disappointments, particularly in men. I know that she *loves* men and *despises* them at the same time.

Deena was bringing Brandon by so Kara could see him. He was four months old, and she hadn't seen him yet. Kara was so excited that she left a message for Deena.

Later on, we got a panicked call. Deena was crying hard, saying, "I can't believe it! He took my baby! I would never do this to him!" I asked her to explain. Morgan didn't want Kara to see Brandon because he and Kara had a falling out during a time when Morgan and Deena were going through some domestic violence. I wanted to comfort her, but God made me give her the truth.

I said, "Deena, I know exactly what that feels like. I can believe this, because your daddy ran off with you and your sister, too. I was separated from my family. You were separated from your family, and now Brandon is separated from his family. What are you prepared to do?" Then I told her to quit pacifying his needs and tell Morgan the truth—that his issue is not with her family. "It is how he treats you, and we don't approve." I told Deena the truth would stir up the truth.

She listened quietly as if she didn't know how I understood everything. I explained to her that I have clutched my children in the physical sense and the spiritual sense for many years. I told her she must decide for herself and look at the long-range picture. When Morgan brought Brandon home, she came by the house with the baby and I brought Kara home with me.

Last night I went to bed housed in yesterday's fears. I don't know exactly when it was, but I know I asked over and over again for God to give me a new beginning, a new door to open in my life. Sometimes, I have to really think through the things that I ask God for, because He does answer prayers. I need to be specific about what I want, and what the cost may be. I will honor whatever new start God gives me.

One of the doors that was opening was the door to the little girl of the past. I see her stepping through the door. Parts of her are liberated, and she is ready to see and hear the truth, and bring closure to her unspoken pain and suffering. As that door closed, a new door opened—the door of forgiveness.

I sometimes fall into the state of mind of that sixteen-year-old girl again, wondering why am I still being rejected? What about me is so unlovable that no one wants to go the whole journey? Whose failure is it if it's always happening to me? My daughter Sharon saw my depression and kept insisting that I talk to her. She asked me if I was the same person as I was when I was young.

My reply was, "Huh?" I think this morning that I have a better understanding of what she was saying. It comes down to the seasons of time again. Even though my circumstances and choices may look the same, I am different. I have grown up. The truth hurts, but in my youth, I would take my guy back no matter what he had done to me, even if he didn't change, because I was so needy. Today, I need the Truth. I will not allow myself to accept less than the value God said I am, because my neediness doesn't run my life, God does. I have decided that I am waiting for the right husband, and I've learned that I am worthy, and that intimacy is not about sex. Intimacy must come first. I don't want to sleep with a man before we are married, or with another man after.

I removed my wedding ring Vince bought me and gave it to Sharon because I had told her that one day it would be hers. It came sooner than later. The second ring from the renewal of our vows I moved to my right hand and later took off, and yes, I am now free, but we are not yet divorced. The Lord won't let me out now. The down side to being free is that one day you have to make another choice. Will three times be a charm?

It's been a very trying week. I would like to go somewhere and sit down and live in a fantasyland, but it's too late. I've already been living in a fantasyland, and now it's time to live in the real world. I awoke one morning feeling pretty good. I had a good time praying with the Lord on my way to work. I greeted one of my co-workers, Joan. I don't know why but I'm always drawn to her. When I first began to work there, she reached out to me, trained me, and began to install a Godly wisdom into me. She has been there for me through the storms right there on the job.

This morning was like no other. We began to talk about family relationships and my looking for a place to live. She brought up the subject that she and her two children one time had to move in with one of her sisters, and even though her sister had a spare bedroom, she had them sleep in the living room on a mattress. When I looked at the pain in her face, I could see and feel the hurt. I had to stop and take a deep breath. I too had done the same thing to my mother Brenda when she lived with me. I began to see that it was not right, and at that moment, I went over to Joan and asked her if I could hug her for her sister. She hugged me, and I believe she received the spirit of healing, and so did I. She went on to say that her sister told her she wasn't being cruel, she just didn't want her to get too comfortable, because others had taken advantage of her. Joan said it gave her the will power she needed to only be there a short time.

I knew then that I owed my mother an apology. I thought she had gotten too comfortable staying with me for the last four years, so when I moved she came with me, but I only offered her the couch instead of the spare bedroom. It was my way of expressing my hidden anger toward her, and it was inappropriate.

I'm leaving for St. Louis soon, and I can't wait to hug her and ask her to forgive me for my bad judgment. I also plan to talk to her about her childhood and all the things that happened to her. Like many in my family, she can be evasive. Especially when difficult conversations come up, you will see her defensive side, and it ain't pretty, but neither is mine! I am expecting to also connect with some bitter roots in the family, things that affect me but that I didn't create. (*Family curses!* Sin passed from generation to generation.). My eyes are open. I can see things I never wanted to look at before, partly because I have some evasive issues too, and instead of dealing with truth when it's there, I put the responsibility on the other person. No longer am I willing to do that. No more festering or trying to fix situations. It is not my responsibility to fix anything, not even myself. If I allow God in there, He will do all the fixing for me.

I awoke this morning to a dream I've had often over the past six years. It used to bring me such joy—I would wake up feeling loved, desired, and cherished. The dream was about my wedding day. I'm floating down the aisle to the altar. and I look up and I see Vince waiting there looking like a scared peacock, with his hair standing up. Pastor Lee leans over and whispers something to Vince. He smiles, and our eyes meet. My mind is filled with images of him becoming a part of my life, beginning with God telling me that this is the moment you've been waiting for all your life. I feel free to love him and not feel guilty about it. We glide through the ceremony, the rings, and the vows, and the moment when I throw my arms around him is an experience of pure love. It feels eternal, and I know I would never let him go. Love would take us through. It's the ultimate bride's fantasy dream.

However, this morning at the end of the kiss when we hugged, I felt a plunge of a knife in my heart. The sharp pain woke me up, and reality set in. I began to weep. I felt disgusted, and betrayed, and overwhelmed with rage. I'm not who I used to be. I've lost my dream.

I do have a consistent friendship with Elder Pete, who used to go to my church. He has been the only man that God has allowed me to see regularly, sharing meals and conversation. We take turns paying. We are intimate friends but not romantically involved. I'm not interested in him like that. I can open up and cry and be totally honest, and he will pray with me, support me, and give me God's word, and not his own opinion.

It was the night before my trip to St. Louis, and my house was full of empty and half-packed boxes in every room. Everything was in shambles. My load weighed heavy, and I was worn out. I didn't know when or how, but I had to move. The house on Fifty-Fifth Street was haunting me with memories of my marriage and raising my children there. I used to keep the mementos of my marriage on display—my bouquet, toasting glasses, framed marriage license, wedding pictures, everything I valued about being married. Now I was being tormented by them, reminded of my failed marriage, and I had to go. I packed up everything.

I wanted to take a copy of the book I was working on to St. Louis in case I stumbled upon a publisher, so I went to the library to print out my disk. Months of hard work had disappeared. My disk was fried. I *flipped*. I went outside and my daughter and my car were gone. I *flipped again*. I began to walk down the street with my granddaughter and her friends. My daughter drove up, and I asked her to take the kids and meet me at home. It was a long three-block walk at an angry pace.

After arriving home, I began to rant and rave about everything in my disastrous life. I was being beaten down from every direction. I called Julie and got her answering machine. I left a panicked message. Then all of a sudden…a peacefulness came over me. It was not my book I was trying to publish, but God's book, and I knew that everything was going to be okay. I let everything about my life and home go. The trip ahead was an old vision but unknown journey.

I have a desire to surrender fully to God's will, and I am still learning how to do it. It is a moment by moment, breath by breath process; it is determined by my thoughts and my beliefs, whether I am operating from my Spirit or my flesh.

Today, I got on the plane and had a peaceful sleep. I am grateful for the rest, because I didn't know what was coming. I had no plan; I just knew that I was led there. After arriving, I went to the baggage claim to get my luggage. I was surprised that I didn't see my family waiting for me. After all, it had been eleven years since I had been there. I went outside and waited at the curb. After a very long time, I started scrambling for change to make a call. All my fears began to surface. I started talking to myself.

"This is the reason why I never came back to this town. These people are out to get me. That's why they sent me away. I wonder if I can turn around and take a plane home." I decided to ignore the voices, and went back inside to page my mother. Shortly after that, my sister Aritha and her son appeared. It occurred to me that perhaps they thought that I was at Southwest, but I had come in on American West. Unfortunately, it's a stigma that black people always fly on Southwest, and sure enough, that's what she thought. I was glad to see her.

I had the opportunity in St. Louis to sit down and study my family. I really wanted to understand them, in hopes of understanding myself better. It's still so many things inside of me that's not like the Lord, and I got a chance to see that too. My sisters were so rowdy and bad to the bone! They were also gentle, accepting, loving, and willing to forgive and move on. They have learned to look past yesterday. They were beat down and still could get up and forgive. I saw this with how they treated my mother. The rough parts of me that don't glorify the Lord surely came out on my visit, and I knew that I was related to them. It has been said that a family that prays together stays together, but with my siblings, it's more like a family that plays together gets enraged together.

LET THE HEALING BEGIN

My second day there, I had a strong impulse to visit the old neighborhood on Maffitt Street. To my surprise when I arrived, the house where I had lived was no longer there, just an empty lot full of grass and broken boards. It was fenced in. I looked through the fence and got a visual picture of where the old apple tree used to be where Grannie Gran would pick apples and make us pies. I stood there for a minute focusing on where the old rusted car had been parked. I closed my eyes and thought about the different times that Kent had taken me there. I remember the view looking out of the car's front window into the back window of the house, wondering if someone was going to see us or come and help me. But no one ever did.

I pulled out my camera and began to take photos of the lot. There was a large man lying on the back of a pickup truck parked on the street next to the lot. He said, "Hey! What're you doing? Why are you taking pictures?"

I explained to him that I grew up in the house that used to be there. He asked me my name and I told him. "La Wanda."

He smiled and said, "You don't remember me, do you?"

I replied, "No."

He said, "My name is Keith Adams, and I used to live directly across the street from you."

I began to laugh because as God gave me a recall memory of this neighbor. I remembered him because I had had a crush on him when I was a kid. He also had a crush on me. We would exchange smiles and waves, innocent and healthy flirting of two kids. I remembered that I thought, *His mama would never let him get off their porch.*

Then he laughed, and at the same time he said, "Mama would never let me off the porch!" We both had a big laugh and a hug, and we talked about the old neighborhood and the people we knew who lived there.

When I was ready to leave, he mustered up enough courage to tell me that he was off the porch and maybe we could go for ice cream.

Seeing 4014 Maffitt Street got me thinking about Auntie Cedra's testimony that she had given me before I left California. It took me a while, but I finally got up the nerve to listen to the tapes. Her voice was full of anger, disappointment, and sometimes rage. She expressed a feeling of "others got, and I didn't!" She showed animosity toward me, my children, and anybody who got Marie's attention or the attention of loving adults, who she expected to be concerned and responsible for her when she was a child. Her experiences growing up on Maffitt Street were similar to mine but worse; both her brothers did awful sexual things to her.

It lasted longer and was more devastating because she had no escape. She described the house as "a shack," and she always wondered why her mother Grannie Gran would never do anything about the condition of the house, or check on who was coming in and out of the house, or and what was taking place there. She described her first memory of being molested. Her greatest hurt was that he used to throw a nickel on the dresser afterward. She remembered thinking, *Is this all I'm worth?*

After the first time her brother abused her, she said she went downstairs to tell her mom, but Kent was in bed with her mother. He rose up his head and looked at her, as did her mother. At that moment, in her child's eyes, she thought that her mother was also a perpetrator, and she was afraid to speak. From that moment on, she never told her mom about herself and Kent.

From that moment on, she prayed that God would put her to sleep and that she would sleep so sound that she would be dead when Kent came in and fondled her or made her do things. Even as a child, she became aware that she was not the only victim in the house. She suspected that he touched my mother, Brenda, (their sister). She knew about me because she saw him take me to the same places that he took her. She told me that she told her mother about Kent and *me,* but her mother, like many other mothers who are caught in the middle between their children and a molester, refused to believe or acknowledge it. She said she knew that she didn't stand a chance if they didn't believe or do something about me. So she kept everything to herself.

Over the years, Auntie Cedra's children's behavior has changed toward me. I take their word when they tell me something, or they say they are available to do something, but when the time arrives, they often let me down. At first, I could not see the connection or why it continued to happen. Now I understand that the spirit, whether it's positive or negative, portrayed by a parent will fall on a child. It becomes a part of who they are, and they don't even know why. For so many years, Auntie Cedra has loved me and also despised me. It is her belief that I was treated better than her and that my children were treated better than hers. Even though Cedra stepped in to take care of my children during my days of my addiction, she held a resentment that stemmed from her childhood. It affected me and my children and her and her children.

Auntie Cedra recalled another incident that still remains fresh in her mind and heart. She said that she called Marie to tell her she needed some food for my kids, and Marie brought her a twenty-five dollar check. Cedra became enraged when she spoke of this, saying she still had that twenty-five dollar check, and what was twenty-five dollars going to do? She went on to say that at Christmas time Marie brought over numerous expensive gifts for my children and brought her children socks.

"I can buy my own socks!" she said angrily, with her face all curled up.

I didn't know how to respond, so I continued to listen to many other negative stories in which she showed her pain and her feeling of being less than, left out, a victim, cheated and unloved by the adults who should have been aware of what was going on inside her. Auntie Cedra gloated in her interview when she spoke of running away from home and telling the juvenile authorities that she didn't want to go home. She didn't really tell them why, but she was adamant as her mother sat across the table smirking, sure that no secrets would be revealed. In those days, no one told family business! Today, it is expected for children to expose unhealthy behaviors. We teach them to recognize "bad touch/good touch" and to tell anyone and everyone about inappropriate touching, candy lures, and suggestive conversation. We tell them to keep telling and telling until someone believes them and puts a stop to it.

As Cedra sat there in the police station, to her surprise her dad, Papa Lum, walked through the door. She only wanted to go home with him. So that's where she went. She loved it. His wife treated her kindly and she had brothers and sisters. Of course, she wanted to stay and live there, but she had to return back to the shack on Maffitt. She was afraid. She never told her father, but as an adult, she wished she had.

Her husband, Uncle Gill, is a godsend for her and her children. It's not often that women with ready-made families and a lot of hang-ups find husbands who stay with them through thick and thin. Although Uncle Gill knew in parts what had happened to her as a child, he loved her and her children anyhow. I could see a brightness about her when she spoke of him. She talked about how uncomfortable she felt whenever any man would go into her daughters' rooms. She expressed at times she couldn't sleep because she needed to keep watch over her daughters at night. After reading parts of the unfinished book, Auntie Cedra stopped talking to me and instructed her family to do the same.

I have decided to put aside my pride. It's never done me much good anyway. The things I should be embarrassed about I talk about, and the things I should talk about I keep hidden. I picked up the phone and dialed Auntie Cedra's phone number. I felt relieved that Uncle Gill answered, because it would buy me some time. He sounded excited to hear from me. We talked about the book and my expectations of what God is going to do with it. He explained to me that he had no "take" on the book; he only hoped it would make money so he could borrow some! However, he did share something with me about himself that I didn't know. He said that he named his son after his stepfather who had come in and taken care of his mother who had nine children of her own. That gave me a better understanding of how he could step into a ready-made family. Auntie Cedra wasn't home, so I asked him to tell her I'd called and to call me. In less than ten minutes, my phone rang and she said, "Is this La Wanda?"

My heart was pounding—finally the silence between us was over. I said, "Yes." The words that followed cut me like a knife.

She said, "Don't you *ever* call my house again!"

I said to myself, *Lord,* and I hung up. Of course, I usually like the last word but in my experience, my last words usually hit people's voicemail. I learned to do that well with the breakup with my husband. I immediately dialed her back, and I had my last word.

I told her voicemail, "You are a wicked woman, scared of change, but the book will be written anyhow! And you will live to regret those words!" And I hung up. That's what pride gets you!

I was sitting at the table at Grannie Gran's house, feeling overwhelmed by all the pictures of Kent in his Army uniform. She had those pictures of him spread out as if she was cherishing his dead "honorable" memory. Even though I knew she was sick, taking dialysis three times a week and chemotherapy once a week, she looked in better health than me. I was sitting there contemplating if this was the day that I would say what I came to say.

I looked at Lavita and then I looked into Grannie Gran's eyes. I mustered up my courage and said, "I need to tell you something before I leave town, and tonight is the night." I couldn't keep my eyes on her. I turned my head and looked at my sister Lavita. Somehow, she knew what was going on. She nodded her head. I had to make sure that I didn't dishonor or disrespect Grannie Gran. I focused forward and put all my attention on Lavita. She became my eyes to watch the expressions of Grannie Gran's face. I began quietly, forcing the words out.:

"One time something terrible had happened to you, and the house was in chaos. You were going to the hospital and we children were left with Kent. He gave us dinner, put us to bed, and then later he came and got me out of my bed and took me upstairs to the bathroom. He would make me do sexual things to him." I began recounting my encounters with Kent using explicit language because I wanted her to get a clear picture of a little girl being exploited by a grown man and being too frightened to tell.

"He would take me under the back porch or in that old car near the apple tree, and he would molest me ..."

After I finished I looked over at Grannie Gran. I was not looking for an answer or a reason why or even her opinion. I just wanted her to hear me. She had the same smirk on her face. She jerked her head to the side as she said, "I never heard of such things."

At that very moment, her daughter, and Lucius Sr. came in. Truth walked through the door, even though I didn't realize it at the time. Crystal had a big smile on her face when she saw me. I had hoped our time apart had softened her to me, but I could see her hard exterior, as if she had a shield up. She didn't speak to Grannie Gran or hug her. I could feel the tension in the room. She threw her arms around me and hugged me. I was relieved to see her and see for myself that she was drug free—despite the rumors in the family.

Grannie Gran seemed nervous and a bit anxious. She didn't have that smirk on her face now. Crystal suggested that she, Lavita, and I go for a walk, and we all left together. In the meantime, Grannie Gran, Crystal's daughter, and Lucius Sr. went shopping. As we walked, we talked about Crystal's children and her change in lifestyle. She expressed that the Lord had been good to her. I told her about my book and my own life's changes. She immediately told me that she had some stories for the book. I hadn't expected that. She began by saying she was molested when she was young by two men. One of them was a loan shark who was close to the family and used to loan them money. The second was Lucius Sr.'s son; we called him Sam. He is dead now; he died very young of unexplainable causes. She said that she told Grannie Gran, and nothing ever happened. The ironic thing about that is that I never told anyone, so mine was a hidden rage. She told and when nothing was done about it, hers became an outrage.

On that walk with Crystal, she also told me that in her drug addiction she had done sexual favors for Lucius Sr. I asked her if she was aware of the rumors that Lucius could be her daddy. Her response to me was, "La Wanda, I am forty years old. Don't you think I know that?" I felt her anger in that, revenge, pay back, but I don't know if it was to hurt her mother or herself by her involvement with him. I'm sure that her drug addiction also played a major part in it. This was very difficult for Crystal, because her and Lucius's daughter, Kelly, are very close. Crystal had not told Kelly any of this, but she said she needed time to tell her the truth.

At the present time, Crystal lived in the house with Lucius Sr., Kelly, Lucius's wife, and Crystal's daughters. I asked her was she afraid to have her daughters around him. She said that she has talked to her daughters and told them exactly what kind of man he is, and to be aware and stay away from him. She said that she was living with him for convenience, but since she no longer uses drugs, she was no longer vulnerable to his advances. If he brings it up, he tries to say how he has helped her, and she reminds him that she sucked him off for that help. The one thing I admire most about her is her real grit. She's not embarrassed or ashamed. It happened and even though she still has to deal with him every day, she keeps moving. She won't let it stop her, but I could feel her pain, her need to be released from her childhood and move on.

When we came back, Grannie Gran, Crystal's daughter, and Lucius Sr. had returned. We were walking towards the apartment complex. I could hear her walker banging the ground every fourth step. It banged with such intensity, I could hear the fear in it, the reality, and the secrets, but I didn't hear her release. The denial was still there.

Lucius Sr. didn't have anything to say, but I knew he knew something. He had been the third man in Grannie Gran's life for at least forty years. I could feel his shiftiness, unspoken words, but his eyes were what gave him away. Not only had this man portrayed a lying image to his family and the world, he also held Grannie Gran's secrets, as if they were partners in crime.

Later on that night, Aritha, me, my mom (Brenda), and Lavita were sitting in her bedroom with a couple of glasses of wine, and we began to open up. I turned on the tape, not wanting to rely on my own memory of her testimony. Aritha was ready to talk, and I was ready to listen! Her quiet voice began to speak, telling about Ted Jr. She said that when she heard the newswoman Robin Smith come on TV at nighttime, she knew Ted would be coming to quietly pick her up out of bed and take her outside and down the steps to the cubbyhole in the basement under the porch. Our mother worked nights at Track's Lounge, and it left us vulnerable. *That porch again!* It seems it was a theme to the women in the family. When I think about that painful porch, I often wonder why the men and their little girls never ran into each other—maybe they had worked out a schedule. *What was it about that cursed porch? Did they know what each other was doing there? Who started it? Why?*

Aritha was about only three years old, but she remembers it vividly. She accredits it to why she became so promiscuous at age five. When her cousin Dante used to come over to play, they would sneak down to the same spot and have sex. He didn't force her—she initiated it, and it went on throughout their childhoods and into their teen years.

As Aritha kept talking about her childhood, different scenarios would come to my head. I would have flashbacks and memories of her father's grandma's house across the street—Grandma Lucky. I recall that she lived on the first floor bottom part of the house, and his mother, Madea, lived upstairs. Now she would allow the kids to be at her house sometimes, but before they could make it upstairs, they would have to go through the ridicule of Grandma Lucky. Aritha began to talk about our brother Baggs (Rob Jr.). She said one day they were crossing the street and Grandma Lucky stood up from her green swing on the porch and told them once again, "Git yo dirty black butts across the street!"

Baggs got up the courage to yell back, "Shut up, you blue headed witch!" Back in those days, old ladies dyed their white hair gray but it came out blue. "I came to see my other grandma," he continued. We all laughed, and it took the pressure off.

Out of all my siblings, I remember Baggs the most. I remember holding him when he was a baby. He was very dark skinned, and I was very light skinned. One day I told my mother that we needed to give him a bath because he was dirty. Everyone laughed, and tried to explain to me about skin tone. I insisted that they give him a bath, and so they did. In my little mind, after his bath, he was lighter. He used to like to carry around paper bags, neatly folded, sometimes with toys or his army men in them. I also remember holding him when Rob Lee, his father, was beating Mom in the street. I remember trying not to look, and to hide his face so he wouldn't see.

Baggs turned out to be bisexual and contracted AIDS. I saw him as a victim, too. He certainly was abused physically. When he was first diagnosed with AIDS, I was told he was shunned by the family, but as he got sicker, they took care of him at Aritha's house. I talked to him on the phone when I first got saved. I wanted him to receive the Lord Jesus before he died. I didn't have money for the plane fare, but I got a bus ticket. It took me three days to get there, and when I arrived, all of my family was at the bus station to greet me. I was anxious to go see Baggs, but they told me he had died the day before I got there. That was probably better for me, because my memories of him would continue to be of him as a healthy child. I sat down on the bench and wept.

His homegoing was the first real family function with my siblings since I've grown up. We all wore the same outfit, a yellow dress with a black jacket. We all sang (badly), but I'll never forget the song. "We are Going to See the King, Hallelujah, Hallelujah, Hallelujah …" Years later, we were talking about the funeral when Grannie Gran said, "Wow! That was some horrible singing!"

I said, "Grannie, I was part of that crew!" She chuckled.

Aritha said, "Before Grannie Gran moved off of Maffitt Street, everyone could come around, but when she moved to Florrisant County, they were not welcome."

I looked at my mother, Brenda, sitting across the room, and it was one of the rare times that she wasn't being defensive or making excuses. She was sitting quietly but stiffly, as if this were not her life we were talking about. Anger began to rise up in me, and I shouted, "No wonder she's over there shaking like a boot! Why did she let them treat her like that? And why did she let them treat her kids like that?" I wasn't looking for her to answer. I was just lashing out with my anger.

Suddenly I caught myself and looked around. The Christian part of me stepped in. I lowered my voice and apologized. I tried to explain that Mom was being passive aggressive, and she needed to start standing up for herself.

I went on to say that if they had just done something about the abuse, perhaps we all could have turned out different. Most of us are not really nuts; we're just portraying symptoms of pain because of the abuse. Parents are supposed to protect their children and prepare them for the journey. We were robbed.

Aritha's willingness to open up and talk about what happened to her was helpful to all of us, but especially to Vita. Her hearing Aritha's stories about their abuse by her father Bean helped her begin to connect to her own feelings about him. She had this love/hate for him, which she never had explored. She was quiet like Mom, but she was listening.

Aritha was used to anger. She often was the recipient of anger from many directions—her mother's boyfriends. She grew up with the feeling that nobody loved her and her siblings, or cared what happened to them. Memories burn in her mind of her and her siblings being abused by Bean and Shane, Brenda's second and third husbands. Bean was there for six sick years, and Shane was there for ten years. Nikki was the baby when Bean came along, so she escaped a lot of the abuse, but she caught hell from him later on when she lived with him. Vita was his daughter by Brenda, and Baggs, Stephen, and Keggy were the boys. All the kids were by Rob Lee Sr., Brenda's first husband, except me.

Aritha began to tell me a story right out of a horror movie. She said Bean put four nails up over the wooden sliding doors in the living room. In all her life, she'd never seen nails as big as those were. She said she doesn't remember when he put them up, or what drove him to such madness, but there was one nail for each child. Later he put up a fifth nail for Nikki. He would hang the children up on the same nail each time as if their names were on them. Then he would throw open the sliding doors and begin to beat them from all sides as they hung there. Aritha remembers being awakened out of her sleep, along with her siblings, and being hung up and beaten regularly. Afterwards, Mama Brenda was ordered by Bean to rub the children with alcohol. I asked Aritha what was Brenda's response. She said, "Girl, like always, nothing. She had that blank look on her face." She always did what she was told to do. She would fight for herself, but not for the children. In fact, she used to tell on them to get herself out of trouble. At least that's how it looked to Aritha.

Aritha remembers when her mom was married to Shane, her mama's third husband. She was married to him for ten years until his death. He would display a lot of meanness and hot temper towards the children. One night they went outside to play. They were having fun, and it began to rain, so Shane screamed out the window for them to come in. They didn't want to come in, so they didn't. She said that she had to go in to go to the bathroom. The long stairwell was dark, and as she reached the top of the steps, Shane jumped out and began drilling on her like she was a grown man. He kicked her, punched her, and cursed her. She got away from him and ran down the street to Maffitt, where Grannie Gran lived. She ran into the house, breathing hard and crying and screaming to the top of her lungs, "Look what he did to me! Shane beat me up!" As she stood there bleeding Brenda was coming up the steps. She entered the room and started saying, "Shane did not do that to her!" Aritha was so upset because Brenda hadn't even been there to see it, but she took up for him.

Aritha felt she wasn't getting anywhere with Grannie and Brenda, so she ran down the steps, across the street to her other grandma's house. She told me, "You know I had to be desperate to run there." Her uncle Ralph was there. He grabbed the hatchet and drove his truck to Aritha's house, but Shane was gone. Aritha's only sense of relief was that at least someone took her side and believed her.

I asked Aritha a second question. I wanted so badly to find some kind of excuse for my mother. I asked her, "Do you think she was scared of him?"

Aritha told me bluntly, "No. Whenever they got into it, she would fight him back."

Not only was Shane abusive to them, but his mama would come over and soak them in a tub of hot water and then beat them with an extension cord. Mama Brenda never had much control over the children. She didn't know how to discipline, so she relied on the methods of her boyfriends and their mothers. Brenda often said to the children, "I'm going to call your grandma over here to whup you."

Aritha remembers the last time her mother said that to her. She got up enough courage to tell her mother, "If you don't whup them, ain't nobody else whupping them no more." The beatings stopped. She was fourteen and pregnant and tough enough to stand up for herself—and everyone else.

WHAT'S DONE IN THE DARK COMES TO THE LIGHT

The day had come and it was time for Aritha to face Baker Boy's family. With a little push from me, she was ready and willing to tell her story. I called his wife Judy and her daughter Joy was there. I told them we would like to come and visit. On the way, we got lost. It was a gray area and I wasn't even driving. We arrived and pulled up in front of the house. Baker Boy's sons were standing outside on the lawn, drinking. We made eye contact, and the guys who were involved knew why we were there. It was a moment that I knew was out of my control, but the Lord's power was there. We all greeted each other and hugged—it had been many years since we'd seen each other.

We went into the house, and the guys followed us. There sat Judy, Baker Boy's wife, still as beautiful as she was twenty-five years ago. She had light brown skin and no wrinkles, and her smile was open and inviting. His daughter was there, too. We used to spend a lot of time together, hanging out when we were kids. One thing I missed when I left St. Louis as a child was being with Joy and Kat, her sister. I threw my arms around her. She was still very small, but had a heart of gold, along with her mother's warm smile. I almost felt guilty for what we were about to do, but I knew it was necessary.

Baker Boy's sons' wives were sitting in the living room as well. We didn't feel the need for them to leave. They were a part of the family, now, even though this happened before they married. We made small talk for a while, trying to put everyone at ease, including myself. I began by talking about the house on Maffitt Street. I asked them did if they remembered anything unusual about it. They said they remembered how crowded it was, and that a lot of people went through there. It was a central location, and Grannie Gran was watching almost everybody's kids.

I said, "Something happened to me in that house, and I wasn't the only one."

Everyone was quiet. I began telling them my story. The atmosphere began to change. There was a restlessness in the air. I continued to tell my story, wanting to open the door for Aritha's story. When I finished, I looked over at my sister. She was fidgeting. I asked Aritha if she'd be more comfortable if the men left, and she said yes.

With only the women left in the room, Aritha began to speak. At first, she used her little quiet voice, describing her cousins coming to take her and her friend Tia, who was the sister of Aritha's firstborn child's father for a ride. They were about fourteen years old. Aritha didn't know it, but she was pregnant with Paula when all this happened. For the next twenty-five years, Paula's father and his family refused to have anything to do with Aritha or her child. As Aritha went into more detail, her strength began to break through, and her voice got louder. She said Ray and Ron were in the front seat and they were in the back, thinking they were going to the movies. All of a sudden the boys turned down a dark road and parked the car. They told Aritha to get into the front seat. Before she knew what was happening, the boys were stripping Tia's clothes off her, and they took turns raping her. She was crying and yelling, "Stop! Stop! Why are y'all doing this?"

"When the first boy Ron got off of her, I thought it was over, but then I was shocked to see Ray get out of the car and go around to the back seat. These were my cousins and I had trusted them. My mother had convinced us to go with them, especially Tia who didn't want to go," Aritha continued.

They never touched Aritha physically, but made her a witness to their crime. She remembers screaming and pleading with them to stop. But they didn't. She was afraid that they were going to do the same thing to her. She didn't understand why they were doing this thing—especially to family! She knew it was "not right."

After they finished they discussed whether or not they should kill the girls. They said they didn't trust them to keep quiet. They didn't know what to do next, so they took the girls back to Baker Boy's house. Aritha was so relieved to be back where she thought she'd be safe. Baker Boy was sitting on the couch, drunk as usual.

The boys made Tia go directly to the back room. They tied her up to the bed and took turns raping her again. Aritha slipped away and ran into the living room, screaming for help from Baker Boy.

She remembers yelling, "They're raping her! They're raping her!" Baker Boy reached his hand out and began to fondle her breast. She couldn't believe his response to her cry for help. Again Ray and Ron asked the girls if they could trust them. She and Tia had to promise the boys that they would never say anything.

However, as soon as they got dropped off at Aritha's house, they ran in the house screaming about what had happened and calling the boys' names. When Grannie Gran and Brenda heard what had happened, they told Aritha not to tell the police because they were family, and family should take care of family.

A silence fell over the room. It was hard for everyone to look into each other's eyes. I believe the first words came from Joy, who said, "The Bible says that everything that is done in the dark must come into the Light, and it is not meant, no matter who it is, to live in pain" (Job 12:22).

The words *Thank you* fell out of my mouth. I knew that I was in way over my head, but the Lord wasn't. Then Joy went on to say that it was not what Jesus represents...He represents freedom. He wants it even for the individuals who did the hurting. I chuckled because what she was saying confirmed my purpose for being in the room. This is about deliverance and healing—it's not personal. She continued to express herself with power from on high. The men who did the hurting have suffered too because this has been covered up for so long, and the results of it have manifested through their chronic alcoholism and drug abuse.

Joy said she has been led to pray for her family's deliverance and healing from their addictions, but she never understood where these things stemmed from. She and her sisters were sheltered from abuse. They knew nothing about it. At this moment, I knew that Joy and I had a connection in Christ Jesus as well as blood relation. Both of our questions about the family were being answered. I felt weak and drained from the effort to keep going, even though I didn't know where I was headed. Joy's testimony strengthened me so that we could minister to the others in the room who were expressing their shame, anger, pain, and outrage through a heavy silence.

I looked around at their faces. I could see that the truth was sickening to them. I felt I had dropped them into a dark well, and I needed to help them through encouragement of the Word to come out. Aritha had a look of relief and brokenness. She later told me she was glad that Judy finally knew. She didn't even think about herself. In herself letting go, she gained new strength. Her quiet voice still remains, but she's different. Judy's comment was that Baker Boy gave his life to Jesus before he died. She went to a different church than him, but she knew that he was saved.

At that moment I thought about the wives of the guys and how awkward they must have felt. I wanted to encourage them as well. I told them that this happened long, long ago, but we felt they were part of the family and needed to know the history of it. They are a part of the new direction of deliverance and healing of the family. We all prayed together, and I do believe that a family that prays together stays together. As I left I knew that a part of my purpose was done. I hope that together Judy and I can convince some of the men to give testimony to what they knew and did, in order to assist in the healing.

The next day, Nikki offered to cook dinner for everyone—my mom, Aritha, Vita, Nikki's seven children, Nikki's boyfriend, and me. We ate a good meal with barbeque, rice and beans, and cornbread. Somebody made a store run and got the beer, which we needed. It was fun, and we were excited to be with one another after all these years. But of course, we were still there to do a job. After dinner and a couple of beers, I suggested that we "Dingahs" share pleasant memories to help take us to where we were going.

Aritha said, "If I wasn't so messed up maybe I could remember something." We all laughed, and I asked if she was referring to being messed up off the beer, or just being messed up. She said both!

I asked the question, "Is there anybody here who doesn't feel messed up? Are we all damaged?" Everybody agreed to being both damaged *and* messed up. Laughter filled the room.

All the women were still sitting at the table and two of the teenage girls began to clear away the dishes. We invited them to sit down with us, and after they finished cleaning up the table, they did. The mood was still kind of jolly and silly, but I felt it was time to get started with the real business we were there for.

Just then Aritha broke out laughing and said, "Oh, I got a funny story! My daddy Rob Lee used to sell weed. One night he got his package, but he didn't have time to bag it up before he went to work. He just hid it upstairs. When he left our brother Keggie went upstairs and found the weed, and came back downstairs and asked us if we wanted to smoke some weed. We all said yes, of course. Not only did we smoke it, but he was divvying it up into little packages for us. Finally, we went to bed.

"Daddy came home, and there was a knock at the door. A man asked if he could he speak to Keggie. Daddy was like, "What do you want?" He said again that he wanted to speak to Keggie. Daddy said, "No, speak to me." The man said, "Does Keggie got any more of them nickel bags?" Daddy ran upstairs to check his stash. When he saw how much was gone, he beat Keggie's butt." Everyone rolled on the floor and screamed with laughter.

After the laughter, the Dingahs began to reminisce and talk about the horrible beatings that Bean used to give Keggie. He absolutely hated Keggie. His beatings were severe enough to leave physical and mental scars on Keggie for the rest of his life. Keggie went into a really bad drug habit, where he would steal from anybody, even small amounts. He just took and stole, took and stole, with no regard for anyone or anything. His family continued trying to love him and give him housing, especially Aritha. People were always coming around looking for him to kill him over little debts and items. Just recently, he got off dope and was staying with his father Rob Lee. He seemed to be doing better for a while, but then his old habits took over again.

Suddenly Nikki began to cry. She said, "It's just so much! I don't know where to start." I told her to start wherever she wanted to start.

She began, "I was about twelve, and I was sitting in the kitchen with Vita playing cards. Vita got up and went to the bathroom. Bean's brother Ben came in and reached over and grabbed my breast. This is how it always started with men. I knew something was about to happen. I got a funny feeling around certain men, knowing they would approach me soon. He touched my breast again, and I moved away. He said, 'You know what I want to do, and you gonna do it now.'"

"I said, 'What about Vita?'
He said, 'Don't worry about Vita.'"
Nikki said, "It made me wonder did he do this to her too?"
"Vita came back into the room. She had got in some kind of trouble with Bean and was upset, so she wasn't thinking about me. But I was thinking about her and what might be happening to her, too." Nikki took a deep breathe and continued.

"Ben went into the living room and told Bean that he was going to the store, and he was going to take me with him. I was afraid and didn't want to go."

As Nikki was telling her story, now Bree, her fifteen-month-old baby daughter, began to cry loudly. One of the kids brought her to Nikki, who held her and consoled her while she finished her story.

Nikki continued, "I told Ben and Bean I didn't want to go to the store. Bean shouted, 'Nikki, what you mean you don't wanna go!? Here's your chance to get yo butt out of the house, and you don't want to go?' I went and got in the car.

"Ben said, 'See? I told you. I can get you any time I want.' He drove to a deserted street and parked. I said, 'I thought we were going to the store.'"

Nikki paused. She was having trouble getting her words out. She held her baby tightly, as her tears began flowing harder.

"He told me to get into the back seat ..." Just then all hell seemed to break loose all over the house. The children were screaming, fighting, and running into the room. We were all swept up into the emotions. Aritha and Nikki were crying.

"...So Nikki, he told you to get into the back seat of the car?" I knew I had to get her to continue. If she didn't, she would never heal.

Nikki began to speak in such a quiet little voice that I had to say, "Speak up, girl! You and Ritha been silent for so long that you gonna get your speaking voices back and your singing voices back, too."

Aritha said, "I hope so, 'cause I used to prune ..." (We knew she meant "croon.") Everybody laughed, and we all broke out in a chorus of "Going to See the King." It helped to calm the troubled waters.

When the laughter died down, we sat quietly and listened to the sounds of Nikki's children playing and running through the house.

I said, "Nikki, getting back to the backseat of the car. What happened?"

Nikki said, "I thought it was going to be the same old regular stuff that I used to do to my uncles. I didn't want to do it, but I had to...but this time Ben told me to take my clothes off. I thought about it. None of my uncles—Ted Jr., nor Kent—told me to do that. I wondered what he was up to...I just sat there. I told myself, *I can do this*. Just get through it. Just go on and get it over."

I interrupted her and asked her, "Kent did you too?! What did Ted Jr. do to you?"

Nikki answered, "I don't remember Kent raping me. Ted Jr. would...force me to do oral sex."

Aritha blurted out, "Like that? Ted Jr. used to be on top of me. I can remember at that time I didn't know that what he was doing to me was called penetration. I'd be listening to Robin Smith news broadcast."

I then asked Nikki, "Where did Kent get you from?"

She said, "He'd get me from my bed in the back room at Grannie Gran's house."

I went on to ask her if she knew anything about the cubbyhole under the steps. It took her a minute to remember that, but she said he mostly used to take her into the basement. It was dark down there.

Aritha said, "Yeah, the cubbyhole! I remember it!"

I tried to joke, "It must have been *the* spot." Everybody tried to laugh.

The next words that came out of Nikki's mouth struck fear into me: "It really got rough with me when I was in California and Ted Jr. got me."

My heart began to pound, and I said, "Ted Jr. got you in California?!" The quiet still voice in me was saying, "Please Lord, not in my house...not on my watch." I prayed I hadn't been that careless.

She said, "Yeah...at Uncle Mick's house. Uncle Mick was never like that.

Aritha said, "Yeah, you right."

Nikki continued, "He would call me into the room..."

I broke in again, "Let me ask you, why didn't you tell anybody in California? What were you afraid of?"

Her response was, "All I could think about was why am I here? Why am I not with my mama? Why did she send me away? Why can't I live with my daddy? He had all his other kids, why not me too? Everywhere I go there's all these men wanting me to do the same things ..." She began to break down and cry. "Why did I just have to deal with this alone? Nobody understood." She took deep sobbing breaths. She was on a roll, and she was letting it out. "I used to say to myself, *It's okay, it's okay.* I've gotta do it, this is what we're supposed to do. It's bad, but I gotta do it...Ted Jr. wouldn't even come to me all the time. I was going to him!"

I broke out into a loud cry, and we all just cried together. We were screaming and bellowing in pain, pleading before the Lord.

"I got used to it," Nikki said through her tears.

I knew that rape victims' bodies sometimes responded to the act, but that didn't mean that they weren't violated. I shared that with her. I wanted her to not feel ashamed. There was no shame for us, because we were children. The shame was in the adults who did it and those who did nothing about it.

We looked over at our mom. She was just sitting there with her blank look on her face she always has.

I said, "So Nikki, finish your story about Ben."

Nikki was quiet for a minute, gathering her thoughts. She said, "Anyway...Ben told me again to take my clothes off. So I did." In between short breathes, Nikki recounted the rape. "I began going down on him. He said he didn't want that, that he wanted me to turn over like a dog. He began to force himself into me. I broke into tears and cried, 'Why are you doing that? IT HURTS!' He didn't go in all the way, but it still hurt. When he finished, he gave me a towel to wipe off. I remember bleeding and crying. He told me to get used to it, that's the kind of thing that girls like me do in life. When I got back home, I didn't tell Daddy Bean. I was scared he would beat me and say I was telling lies on his brother.

"Ben took me for rides a lot after that. He always penetrated me from the back. It only stopped because I ran away. Daddy Bean put me into a group home for twenty-one days. I told the people there that I had been hurt and violated. They sent me back to St. Louis. Nobody ever pressed charges back then."

I asked Nikki, "Did you ever try to tell your mom about what happened?"

She said, "No. I was just glad it was over."

Aritha began to speak again. "I remember the day you guys moved to live with Bean. Usually Keggie would go for the summer with y'all to Chicago, but this year he wasn't going. Mama kept saying, 'Pack all y'all stuff.' And I kept saying, 'Why? Aren't they comin' back?'

"Mama said, 'Yeah,' but I knew she was lying. Grandma Mattie came over to see us—she was the only grandma that would love and hug on us that I can remember. She knew we were leaving. And soon she left too, to move to California with Marie."

Aritha went on. "She would hold all us kids on her lap and everybody had a piece of her arms. She was always interested in what was going on with everybody, especially when she would come to visit. Nevertheless, we didn't tell her everything."

The room was quiet. Aritha continued, "I was happy when Ted

Jr. married Carrie and went into the Marines. Carrie's mother and father were coming over to visit. Ted Jr. was all dressed up in his Marine uniform, parading around like everything was all right. We didn't get a chance to see her parents, of course, because we were sent to the back room as always."

Mama got up and left out. Nikki shouted toward the house, said, "Mama, where are you?" There was no answer.

I said, "Go and get her."

Nikki went to find her and brought her back. We didn't want her to miss out on any of this conversation.

The drinks had taken effect, at least in Aritha. Every now and then she would blurt out, "Make sure that damn tape is on!" or "Is that tape getting all this?"

I said, "It's on!"

Aritha said, "This mess is all about us. All of us." She began to show her drunkenness and her anger at mom. "If a person is mad, they just gon' be mad. Too bad! This is God's honest truth! The whole lot of us stayed in a dang two bedroom, and there were at least six of us! Bean's upstairs kitchen was a little porch, and that was our play area. There was six dogs living on that porch too. We could never go outside. We was always confined to the porch! Our toys was our school work. All we could do all day long was to play school. This is the truth! One day yo' mama set there just like she's sitting now, and we were all out on the porch with his dogs. He came in from work through the living room—there was a lot of room in there!—straight to the kitchen. Mama's sittin' at the kitchen table, and we out there on the porch...Now remind you, Wanda, these are his dogs. He was a dog lover, and that's why I can't stand dogs today! We had to play in *dog crap*.

"The door was open. Bean looked out on the porch and said, 'You clean up!'

"We got up and started to clean, sweeping and bleaching stuff.

Our brother Stevie stood in the doorway and said, 'Mama, I need something to pick up the trash with.'

"Then Bean said in a harsh and cruel voice, 'Pick it up with your dang mouth!'

"I looked at this man and I knew he was serious, and yo' mama just sat there and acted like she did not hear a thing."

Nikki said, "She didn't even look our way."

Aritha said, "Then I stood up and told Bean, 'They ain't gon' pick up nothing with their mouth! And I ran out the door racing past him and went to find my father."

Suddenly Nikki began to show some feeling. "Mama didn't even look our way. Every man that Mama had would cuss us, and beat us, and—all she would ever say is was, 'Y'all better stop. I'm gonna call Shane or Grandma on you.'" Always referring to Shane's mother in these cases.

Aritha said, "I was scott free. My daddy had come to get me, but I couldn't stay. I had to go back. My brothers and sisters were still there."

Nikki jumped in, "Oh, yeah, and Mama got up to defend us, but as usual it was way past too late. Even today, she does the same thing. The team that's winnin', she's on that side. If for some reason they start losin', she quickly jumps to the other side. You can't blame her though, she's just surviving. She never learned how to do any different...I remember having to go to other people's house to get water! It was embarrassing, and I was ashamed. This happened everywhere we lived with Mama."

I said, "I can remember visiting, and there wouldn't be no heat, no water, or lights in some of those houses, but I was just visiting... And I was just enjoying being with y'all. I knew that Marie would be sending for me or coming to get me. So it didn't affect me like it affected you."

Aritha spoke out angrily, "That lousy Ted Jr., he's goin' to pay for what he did to us!"

"He's already paying," I said. "He leads a wicked life, striving from turmoil to turmoil. He can't seem to get clean of drugs or alcohol. He has no happiness. No peace. In fact, he lives in total darkness."

"He's gonna have to face us one day," Aritha said. "Or at least the truth. What's he look like, abusing little kids?"

I wanted to change the subject. I know what he did was horrible, but the compassion that I felt for him had nothing to do with me. It came from the love that lives on the inside of me. God said, "The book is about healing and deliverance for everyone." That doesn't mean just for the Dingahs.

Aritha said, "And let me tell you something else. Vita and Nikki was living in Chicago with Bean. Me, Keggie, and Paula, my daughter, went to visit them. The first day Bean was nice. He suggested we go to Popeye's Chicken's grand opening. He ordered a lot of food. Then he looked at me to pay. He always worked it so I had to pay. Then when I was broke, he started treating us like dogs again."

I could hear the anxiety in her voice.

She went on, pouring out her pain like a waterfall over a cliff. "Do you know this man made a pot of beans, and we ate off that same pot of beans for three days? His own wife Millie didn't say nothing about that."

Everybody was listening intently, especially Vita. She knew all about her father, but hearing someone else talk about him was shocking.

Aritha took control again. "Rob Lee Sr., my daddy, came to get me, Paula, and Keggie. He had Nikki pack her stuff, too.

"When it was time to leave, Daddy didn't take Nikki. He said, 'Daddy will send for you later.' Nikki was devastated, and so was I. I was so angry with him for that. I believe that the only reason he left Nikki was that he didn't believe she was his child."

I want to share my sister LaVita's story. Some of the testimony she has told me was bizarre and maybe imaginary. She is very creative. It's not for me to judge the story—my purpose is to retell it.

So here it is.

"Living with Dad I liked to be up under Millie all the time. What Mama wasn't doing, her and Daddy was. Nikki went to Millie's sister's house, and Daddy had a friend over, someone he worked with. They were both police. They were sitting at the table, snorting cocaine and drinking, and I was sitting there with them. I was about six. His friend asked Daddy who I was. Daddy was so high he said, 'That's my baby. That's my six-year-old daughter.'

"The friend replied, 'Damn, she's sexy. I would like to git that.'"

LaVita said she ran into another room to call Nikki on the phone to ask her what "git that" means.

Nikki told her, "It's talking about sex."

LaVita got off the phone and went back in the kitchen.

"Nikki probably didn't think anything of it, because she knows I'm wild like that and silly. I have a messed up sense of humor. I told my dad I was fixin' to go to bed. At that time I had a German Shephard named Duke. He always slept in my room. I locked my door, but I could still hear their conversation. After they got snorted out or whatever, my daddy told his friend to go ahead and do what he wanted to with me.

"My daddy unlocked my door and put the dog out. He knew my dog would have bit his friend. Duke didn't play. He was my protector while we lived there.

"It was just like that dash in my back that wouldn't go away. The guy came into my room and raped me. I wasn't in any condition to fight back because I was still sore from my daddy's beating. He had beat me because he said I kissed a boy. He said he drove past and seen me kissing a boy. *Now how the hell can you know what you're seein' if you're all cracked out?*

"Anyway, that man came in, and he did what he wanted to

do. I was already in my nightclothes. Daddy made us put on our nightclothes before we went to bed. When the man finished, he got up, went into my daddy's bathroom to wash himself off and then went back into the front room to snort some more coke.

"I didn't scream for Daddy. It didn't make a difference, 'cause he was playin' music loud, and he couldn't hear me anyway. I don't think he wanted to hear me. I never said anything to my daddy about it, and he never said anything to me. I never told Millie, but I think she knew.

"It was like he sold me, but he really didn't sell me. It was just him and his partner snorting coke together. Usually he never allowed anyone else to touch me.

"I was scared. The only place I wanted to be was with my dog Duke. I figured the man would not come in and take a chance with my dog there. But Daddy put the dog out.

"There was blood coming from my back from where my daddy had beat me. Millie always looked in on me when she came home. She didn't see me so she asked my daddy where I was. He said that I better be in that bed. But I was lying on the floor beside the bed. She came back in and opened my door and said, 'Vita? What's wrong?'

"'My back hurts.' She tended to my wounds. I was so hurt. All the pain that I had been through could not compare to what my daddy had done. I think Millie knew. She had to, 'cause of the way I was acting. In my head, I could never put it together. It's like I was my daddy's baby girl and his only child—why would he let anything or any person harm me?! The only thing my daddy ever did was beat me. The reason I believe he acted like that is because I looked like my mama. I got so many messed up ways like my mama, and my dad really did not like my mama. He would say, 'You are just like your ignorant mother.' I am so mad at my daddy. Period."

As she had told me her story, I watched her swell up in rage. Her voice got harsh and hard, and she began to swear a lot. She began to speak to her father instead of me, as if he were in the room.

She said, "You know me, because you raised me! Now how under God's sun are you going to let another person hurt me? They don't know a thing about me."

Then she leaned forward to me. "My father was a cop, Chicago's finest. I used to have a problem at night when my daddy was at work. I couldn't sleep.

"I was the type to say, 'I'm Daddy's baby. He knows I'm his baby, in his own way.' Do you hear what I'm sayin'? He was just so difficult. He could have got tore up when his mama died. She seen all her kids graduate high school except him. Even though I know what my daddy allowed to be done to me, everybody is entitled to some mistakes.

"He had such pressure on me, it was like living in solitary confinement, cause that's all my daddy's house was. You better not even think about messing up in school. Daddy never played that.

"I'll tell you when I started to lose respect for him. It was when Millie and the school told him I needed to see a psychiatrist. He really went off...And I didn't get no counseling. My daddy, he might be sick in the head, but I knew he was on drugs. Me and my daddy was a lot alike, but we never could see eye to eye.

"Now my daughter—my daddy would never hurt my baby. He would never let anything happen to my child. That thought never crossed my mind. I believe he was trying to make up to her for the things he did to me."

Once again, Vita began speaking to her father's ghost, with her head moving from left to right.

"I'm not the one to judge you. You are my daddy, and the Bible says to obey your mama and your daddy. So whatever you have done to me, I couldn't hurt you because you are my daddy!"

She began to laugh loudly. She said, "I asked God what happened to my daddy. How did he die?"

As I listened to her story, I thought to myself that perhaps she did need a psychiatrist.

It's my last night in St. Louis; Chickie has surfaced. She was looking for a reason to get out. My family seemed to be breaking free of the past, but I felt burdened and bound by their testimonies, and I didn't have a clue on what I should do next. It's not unusual for Chickie to come out during vacations. Usually, I'm far from home and Vince is with me, and she can break free and still be protected. He's probably the only man in my sober life who truly knows Chickie and accepts her actions. That night he was nowhere around, so I tried to assimilate his existence by hiring myself a designated driver with fringe benefits.

It was Friday night, and my sisters and I were going out dancing. We were known as the "Dingah Sistahs." I had been warned that when my sisters drink, they get loose and wild. The difference is I won't drive under those circumstances, and neither will I let anyone else drive me when they're drinking. The driver I hired was a young guy from the neighborhood. I met him when I arrived at my sister Aritha's house. I saw him, I looked, but I didn't think anything about him. However, after being there a week, we were all sitting in the kitchen kickin' it, and I felt some warm breath on the back of my neck.

I had just absorbed a huge blast of reality from my family. I didn't know it but I was looking for an escape. I was needy. Old behaviors surface quickly. I was aware of the sinful nature of my thoughts, but it was too late, because the impulse had moved from my head to my heart. I couldn't make the right choice.

I turned to see where the warm breath was coming from. There he sat behind me, young and fine. My eyes and nose were open. Chickie immediately was working an angle on how, before she had to leave, she was going to score. First, I imagined the innocence of "just a kiss." I invited him to come and be our designated driver for the evening. There was no changing Chickie's mind. I think I was operating out of hysterical blindness, because I went out and bought a short little two piece orange Tina Turner "shake it down, shake it up" outfit, with matching heels.

We all got dressed at my mother's house, then drove over to Aritha's. I knew know the moment that when I stepped out of the car and my foot touched the ground, I was headed for trouble, and I didn't care. Today, I refused to talk about the book. In fact, I had kicked it, tossed it around, and stuffed it in the suitcase. I don't want any more testimonies. I just wanted fleshy fantasy, flashy fun. "Give it to me, I don't care!" I was trying to drown out God's voice.

When "Young Baby" came down the street, I could tell by the way he was dressed he was a kid, but I just looked past that. His youth was what I was counting on. Shamefully, I had full intentions of taking advantage of him. I was looking to fall further. He drove *me* to the club. My sisters knew what was up and they were helping me set him up, so they met us there. He was so young that they didn't want to let him in the club, even with a fake ID, but my brother-in-law Gene got him in.

I bought Young Baby and myself a drink. After one Cadillac, I was ready to experience a little dancing. Unfortunately, I had forgotten to tell my designated driver his job description, which included dancing, flirting, and entertaining me. My first dance was with Gene. I was getting warmed up on the dance floor. Even though I was making some provocative moves, I kept my boundaries with him, even playfully hitting his hand when he reached out once to touch. Gene told Young Baby, "You better go get that!" I could see the fear on that kid's face, but Chickie didn't care. She was past the point of no return. He came and danced with me on the floor.

I was wild with my emotions of rage and seduction. Then I proceeded to work him over. Those eighty pounds that I had shed and the exercising had made me feel limber and light. I was dancing as if I was twenty again, just like "my designated driver." All the older girls in the club were screaming, "Go on, girl, work it ..."

Chickie isn't good at playing games—once she makes a decision she will make it happen. However, Young Baby was resisting. After a second Cadillac, she got bolder. They were playing "Nasty Girl," and Chickie stood up and began to dance provocatively in front of him and everyone else. In fact, I think she gave him a lap dance, one he won't forget. It was apparent that he was not going to voluntarily let her have her way. Once again, this felt to me like rejection.

It was time to go. I got bolder. In the car, I made some sexual suggestions. Young Baby told me he didn't know what it was, he would love to "do me," but he just couldn't. I said I knew what it was, and it was okay. He couldn't touch the anointing. I knew that God had his hand on me.

I asked him, "Can I kiss you?"

He said, "I don't even kiss my girlfriend or my baby mama."

I replied, "I'm not your baby's mama. I'm not your girlfriend. But I am going to kiss you." And I leaned over and kissed him, and he did kiss me back. It felt pretty good, so I did it again.

"I'm not what you're looking for," he said. It was no need to reply.

Young Baby ended up just driving me to my mother's house and going home. The next day I went to say goodbye to everyone in the neighborhood, but Young Baby hadn't showed up on the street yet. I didn't want him to be embarrassed about last night, so when he came out I hugged him and told him thanks for being my designated driver. And I thanked God that He didn't let me completely fall. I left that town untouched in the flesh, just as I came, but there was definitely something different about my spirit.

ALL EYES ON ME

I arrived at church early last Sunday. I was confused. I didn't see anyone outside or inside the church, which was unusual for a Sunday morning. I began to doubt myself and even whether it was Sunday. I was having a gray moment, spacing out. It brought me back to earlier that morning when I awoke feeling confused and baffled. I knew I had been dreaming all night about Vince and the breakup. I kept replaying old dreams in my sleep, knowing that what I was dreaming had already happened, and that I had dreamed it before it happened. Maybe I was trying to re-dream it with a different ending, again.

I dreamed I was standing in a street and it was nighttime. There were a few streetlights, but it was foggy and dark. There were a lot of women around who were connected to some hotel. Vince was being lured by the different women, and he was so caught up in it that he saw me but he didn't acknowlege me. I reached for him and called him, but he didn't respond or didn't want to respond. I felt a great sadness of just being left behind with no understanding of why, and no efforts at reconciliation. I was clueless and fearful again.

I began to cry out to the Lord, saying, "I don't know who I am! I have visions of who I want to be. It's like waking up a different person! I know all the day-to-day things to do, but I'm no longer happy in my choices, either in finances, environment, or in my marriage. The only thing I really am happy about is my children and grandchildren, and my salvation. God, if you don't come and get me, I don't know what I'll do. I know that your Word is true, and You are real. There is something pulling on me, something in the way, and I can't always hear what You are telling me. I can't see You, but I can feel You. The Scriptures tell me that You will never leave me or forsake me, nor put more on me than I can bear."

This is what I am holding on to. My confusion sets in when I operate in doubt and disbelief, and when I watch my circumstances, instead of keeping my eyes on Him. After praying, I felt my confidence return.

I received a phone call. It was Kara. She wanted to know if I would pick up Jody because she needed a break. I told her sure, and she then said, "You don't know, do you?"

"Know what?" I said. She went on to tell me that she had just found out that her boyfriend Russell has been living with another woman for almost two years, and this woman just had an abortion. Kara was pregnant too with his child. I felt like World War II was starting again. The worst part of this was that Kara was at his family's house every day, and her daughter was on the drill team that his mother sponsors. The whole family knew about both women and covered the truth, lying for him. *Where are the family values?* I thought to myself as we said our goodbyes and hung up.

Before I knew what he had been doing, Russell and I had numerous conversations in my living room about what was going on in my marriage, and what he wanted to do in marriage regarding Kara. I felt betrayed and deceived when I heard that he was doing the exact same thing Vince was doing with other women. It feels like watching a horror show, seeing my daughters repeating the same self-abusive behaviors and depressive experiences.

I have a purpose here, and it is to stand for myself and be an example to my daughters. Now I see that all the years of telling the girls not to cast their pearls before swine have no value, if my pearls are sitting in the mud. My eyes are open now from a lifetime of experience in relationships with men, and now I get to see me again through my daughters in my earliest forms of ignorance. Actually, it wasn't so long ago. As I set standards and grow in my self-esteem, my prayer is that my daughters will follow me in this. No more domestic violence. No more cheating men. No more self-loathing or unworthiness.

Now they seem to be working it out, and I'm glad about it. The only advice I had for them was to put Jesus first, like it or not.

There are more lessons about me every day. It's not always pretty, but it's right. I'm still reliving my past through the lives of my children. I see myself in them, over and over, but I'm praying that our endings will not be the same. Sharing our testimonies is a cry of hope for us all.

Sharon is my adopted daughter. My womb was occupied carrying another child, so the Lord sent her by way of another woman. She is my business partner and main support. She has come on board to my twenty-year vision for a business. When I asked for her help, she came through with energy and in the areas where I am weak in business.

She is strong and creative. Therefore, we fight sometimes, but we know our areas of strength and we both take care of business. I laugh sometimes, even though I want to cry, because she's stuck in a space that is so familiar. She often makes the statement, as I did, that "I don't want to tear up my own house." In the Bible, it speaks about women being out of order in their homes. If your house is not built on a foundation of Christ Jesus, it will fall regardless (1 Corinthians 3:11). Mine has. In time, Sharon will arrive in a perfect space prepared for her on top of the right foundation.

It's been difficult concentrating on the book particularly after my trip to St. Louis. I absorbed an overwhelming amount of negative energy into my spirit by listening to the testimonies of the women in my family. Although I knew I was in search of family secrets, I didn't understand the magnitude of pain, guilt, shame, suffering, and denial.

A Revolving Door

My uncle Ted Jr. is nicknamed Trouble by his family, because after giving birth to him, Grannie Gran was paralyzed for a year. Sometimes families don't realize that the nicknames they give their kids have spirits that are attached to them, and often the children will act out what they are called. He became trouble for many women in our family.

I understand now why he is so "troubled." Even though he's tried numerous times to clean his life up, he continues to get clean and then relapse. I can see in him the results of all the little deeds of sin that we do in our flesh, how they come back to haunt us, especially when we try to turn our life around.

Sometimes when we ask forgiveness and the person we've harmed is not ready or willing to receive it, we are unable to put it behind us. We think we need them to accept our apologies and forgive us. This is what I see in him.

Several of the women in the family have named him as a perpetrator of sexual acts against them. I never had that experience with him, and I'm surprised that I didn't see it in him. I've had him around my daughters and their friends. Kara told me that she remembers him listening to the late night news and then coming in to her room with her and her girlfriend. She said that he would put his hand under the covers. The first few times it happened they played "sleep."

One time Kara asked him what he was looking for. He said, "My watch."

She told him, "Your watch is not in here, and if you don't get out of here, I'm going to tell my mother." She didn't have a problem with him after that. What a strong and brave little girl!

Hearing all the stories about him, I'm disappointed. I'm angry. But I still want him to be free. I love him with God's kind of love. Yes, the things he did were horrible, offensive, and changed the lives of many young girls in our family, but I have hope that we all will be healed and delivered from our family's hidden sickness and sin.

Recently he showed up at church looking for me. He was sober, but he looked worn. He smelled bad, and his clothes were dirty. I could see the hurt in his face and the wanting of relief. I knew that he wasn't in any shape for me to question him about his past actions against the women in the family. I felt an overwhelming amount of compassion to reach out to him with God's love. To me at that moment it didn't matter about all the nasty things he did. I just saw someone who needed Jesus. I've been taught that there is no little sin or big sin—it's just sin, and forgiveness is for everyone. All they need to do is ask.

He hugged me and told me he came by looking for me and that he was hanging out on Third and Newcomb in San Francisco, a well-known drug area. Ironically, it's about five blocks from Auntie Cedra's house. He told me that sometimes he just stands across the street looking at her house. I know he's in search of her forgiveness. He's tried by bringing her roses, reaching out to her, but she has a closed heart to him. I'm not saying that he didn't wrong her, but how can we ask for forgiveness and God's mercy if we are not willing to give it? Openness is required.

I said, "God stands at the door of your heart, and He knocks. All we need to do is answer. Our church has a men's Christian recovery home. Why don't you go there?"

He asked, "Could I work and live there?"

"Sure you could. Go talk to the elders over at the men's home."

"Okay," he said agreeably. I had my doubts, but I gave him my phone number, and I invited him to call me. He left carrying a bag of donated groceries that seemed just meant for him.

I know that being on his *side* to some members of the family would seem absurd, since I too was exploited sexually as a child, but not by him. But when God comes into your life and His presence is so real, you can reach out to people—even the ones that you despise or have harmed you—because you want to please God. Therefore, it isn't personal; it is ministry. No matter what you have done, to yourself and others, God is a forgiving God, and He has new beginnings for all who ask.

I had a joyous surprise last Sunday, and it was needed. As I walked into church, there was my uncle Ted Jr., formerly known as Trouble. He was clean, dressed up, and smelling like he was among the living! I threw my arms around him and thanked the Lord that His word is true, because He had told me the next time I saw my uncle it would be different. Just his showing up lets me know that my purpose is true. It's the small victories in Christ that thrill me. After I had introduced him to the elders and ministers the last time he came, he got into a recovery program that was somehow connected to my church. My church family took care of him in a non-judgmental, loving manner, just as they had for me about twelve years ago.

As the story goes, it looks like Grannie Gran was working three men in her life at the same time. Grannie was a swinger! In fact, on my recent trip to St. Louis, she had a poster on her wall that said, "Smile—It's the Second Best thing you can do with your Lips." I was shocked.

I asked her, "Grannie, what's the first thing?"

She grinned and said, "What are you talking about?"

"That poster on your wall! What's the first thing you can do with your lips?"

She said, "Oh, girl, my cleaning lady put that up there."

I said, "So you left it?"

She didn't reply. Her smile faded away.

The three men that I recall seeing in the ten years that I lived there were my grandfather, Ted Sr.; Papa Lum, who was the father of at least three of her kids; and of course, Lucius Sr., who is still in the picture twenty-five years later, masquerading in the same role as friend.

I didn't know a lot about my grandfather Ted Sr., but I can remember the good feeling of being with him as if it was yesterday. This memory seems to come at a time in my life where I am looking for wholeness and using positive past experiences with men as a focus. I am going back to healthy relationships with men, relationships that had innocence and love. Granddaddy used to come and pick me up and take me around the streets and have me dance for his friends, and they gave me money for it. He was proud of me! He taught me a crazy tradition that I still do today: when I first move into a new house I go in and throw money around in every room. I think of it as a welcoming gesture, a blessing. I've been doing it for years, and the reason is it is my connection to my granddaddy, who would throw money around in his house if he knew I was coming, so I could go and find the coins. Then we would stand over the stove with a pot, cooking oil, and popcorn kernels, and I would love to hear the sound of the popcorn popping. I would dance to it! Today I still eat popcorn at least three times a week, although I admit I use the microwave, and not much dancing.

I found out later, though, that he was a dangerous man; in fact, he had to leave St. Louis because he cut someone with a straight razor and people were looking for him. I was not told that; I just knew he was gone.

I had been talking on the phone to my granddad for years. Once, he came to see me. He seemed old. He wore a short gray afro and seemed kind of childlike, almost reminding me of my mom Brenda. However, the love was still there. He sat on the floor with me one night and we talked for hours about his life and my life. I remember the sadness in his face. He had told me he loved Grannie Gran, but he admitted he was a womanizer. Later I found out he sometimes beat Grannie. I believe that even though they were childhood sweethearts, his womanizing and abuse were factors in their marriage not working.

One positive way Granddad learned to deal with his stress was to make ceramics. He was quite good at it. The first pieces he sent me were two big matching hands that I loved and adored, but I don't have them today. I lost them in an eviction, and I'm sorry for that. The second pieces he sent me were a family of four white swans. One of them is broken, but the set still sits on my windowsill in the kitchen.

Granddaddy was very sick; I wanted to go see him but I didn't. He died and his wife had him cremated quickly. My family was enraged with her because she did not include them in the plans.

Another valued relationship is the one that I had with Granddad's mother, Grandma Bonner. She was a very tall, big boned woman. She used V05 Hairdressing in her silver gray hair; it almost looked blue. My earliest memory of learning about God was with her. It was where I also learned to read. She was a Seventh Day Adventist, which means Saturdays were *rough* around her house. It was a day of worship and no meat! However, she read the Holy Bible and taught me to read it to her.

Reading the Bible aloud at such a young age caused the Word to sink into my spirit. I would hear it over and over again, and though I strayed away for many years, I understand why I have such a deep connection to God's word. Thank you, Grandma Bonner! I also remember how she used to make ice cream out of snow. She mixed it with syrup, cream, and sugar and froze it in a silver ice tray. Oh, how I miss Grandma's loving!

Papa Lum was the second man I recall seeing a lot of in Grannie Gran's presence. He would come to the house on Maffitt regularly, or Grannie Gran would go downtown to meet him. She always took one or two children with her—there were so many, she rotated. He was a short, dark brown-skinned man, somewhat heavyset, who always wore gray or black slacks with a white-collar job shirt, like a government shirt. He had a thick, black moustache, and he always had half a cigar hanging out of the side of his mouth. I was always excited when it was my turn to go downtown to meet him. We would shop, eat a fine meal in a restaurant, and he would give me some money, maybe a couple of dollars. It was strange when I went downtown because I would see white people and they looked so different from the people in my neighborhood that it made me curious. Grannie Gran would tug my arm and whisper to me, "Don't stare!"

Papa Lum would always greet me with loving arms and a big smile. I can't recall seeing any intimate exchanges between him and Grannie Gran. She never showed much loving attention toward anybody or anything—except babies. She just knew what to say and how to do things. I remember often going to see him at a fish market where he used to be. It was fun because whenever we saw him we could expect some kind of treat. I don't have one unpleasant memory of him. I lost contact with Papa Lum a few years after I moved to California. I can't even recall if I ever saw him again, but I know that Auntie Cedra and her children had a relationship with him before he died.

A MOTHER'S CRY

This has been a very difficult year for me. I've been stripped of everything that I held valuable (or so I thought). I went bankrupt. My marriage fell apart, and I found out I was not the only "Alice" in the family (in terms of drugs, addictions, sexual abuse, and mental dysfunctions). I must admit that I know now I had a breakdown of sorts, but I was still functioning, going to school, writing, and half way working. The Lord was carrying me.

I wept for almost an hour, and I didn't want anyone to touch me. I just wanted to surrender everything I was feeling and everything I'd been through in my life to the Lord. Ironically, that's the way I felt when I was first saved. I held my hands up and promised to endure. Since the break up of my marriage, I have learned more about my walk and developed a more personal relationship with Christ. Before I was serving Him out of duty, and now it is my desire to serve Him out of joy, love, and pain. Serving the Lord has taken the place of my using men to heal my wounds of rejection and fear. I don't have the physical comfort of a man anymore there, but the presence of God wraps around me. I know He understands. I know there it is an appointed time for me to love a man again, but this is the time for me to return to my first love and only true love which is Christ Jesus. There is safety in opening my heart to the love of God, but there's no certainty in loving a man. I realized while I was on the altar that matters of the heart create difficulty for saved women because we are emotionally centered. We fluctuate depending on our mood, instead of focusing on what God is telling us to do.

I also learned at the altar to surround myself in praise and worship music. It teaches me how to encourage myself. I have a better understanding why alcohol and certain environments don't work for saved people, because they make you vulnerable to your emotions and you get swept up into sinful behaviors. I'm learning to be selfish in protecting my salvation. It is spiritual warfare, and I am fighting for my life, the life of my children and grandchildren, and the body of Christ. I'm being released from the sword of torment and embracing peace, the Lord's peace.

A couple of days later, I was sitting at my desk at work doing data entry, and I reached over and turned on the tape recorder. I thought to myself, *This would be a good day to listen to the tapes from St. Louis.*

My mother Brenda's voice came on. she was the first one that I attempted to interview in St. Louis. Keep in mind I had no idea what I was doing, but that didn't stop me. I began to chitchat with her, trying to get prepared to get into her story. We talked about some of the things that happened with me and Kent. The more I asked her questions, the more evasive she seemed to get. Things didn't make sense, and she pretended to go dumb. I was really frustrated, and I felt like I was getting nowhere with her. I cut the tape off several times during the interview to refocus myself. Eventually, she began to open up.

I had been typing while I was listening, but after a few minutes, I stopped typing because I realized she was talking about being raped and my conception. I had heard bits and pieces over the years from her and others, but there were so many versions of her story that I never felt like I knew the truth. That's probably why I was still asking the same questions I'd been asking since I was sixteen. I was listening when I made the tape, but I was so focused on getting the material that I didn't hear what she was really saying.

It was not unusual for Harmon, my mother's auntie Liza's husband, to take my mother Brenda to Bertha's house to get homemade bread. My mom was fourteen years old, and Grannie Gran told her to get in the truck and go with Harmon. Mom said she put on her jeans and pulled her long hair up into a ponytail and got in the truck. She didn't notice anything wrong. Then she noticed they were in an area she wasn't familiar with. She said all of a sudden Harmon pulled over to the side of the road in a secluded area. He got out of the truck, and he acted like something was wrong with it. When he got back in, he told her to pull off her blouse. She said no. She was not a promiscuous girl and knew that it was wrong. He told her again to take off her blouse. She said no again. He began to take her clothes off. She began to fight and struggle and hit him. She told him, "You're not supposed to do this! You're my uncle!"

His reply was, "Go on and hit me. You can't whup me."

He cut her jeans off, with whatever he had in his hands (she can't remember). She said he must have planned it and got a knife or something while he was out of the truck.

He pinned her down on the seat, and he raped her. She could do nothing but lie there and cry. When he finished he dropped her off at Bertha's house. He told her she better not tell nobody. She said she ran up the steps. She told Bertha what had happened. Bertha called Grannie Gran. She told her how Brenda looked, clothes all torn and her hair messed up. My mom remembered hearing, "She looks *terrible!*"

Grannie Gran said, "Send her home." But Bertha called the police, and they took her home. She remembers going to the hospital, and the doctor said he could "clean her out," but she might not be able to have children if he did. So they released her, and she went home.

During the interview, I kept asking Mom if they ever pressed charges against Harmon. At first she kept saying, "They couldn't find him." As I pried more, she said, "It was my word against his." She was a victim, and she was pregnant, but she didn't know it yet. Then I thought back to my mother's childlike state of mind, and I knew not to press her any more. I am the result of that rape.

My mother was very upset because her auntie Liza didn't believe her. She told her, "You are just fast!" My mother said that four or five days went by, and Liza wouldn't speak to her. Then Liza came to apologize to her. Mom said that she didn't feel like she could ever forgive her for not believing her. Mom decided to prove her story, and she told Liza to call Harmon and to just listen on the phone. "If he does everything I tell him to do, then you'll know I'm not lying." So they called, and he answered.

Mom said, "If you don't do what I tell you, I'm gonna tell my mama, and my grandma what you did to me."

He said, "What do you want?"

She gave him a list of things she wanted left on the porch, and told him to leave some money in an envelope in the mailbox, and "not no little money either!"

Liza and Mom watched out the window as Harmon did what he was told. The truth was known. But charges were never brought against him.

I turned off the tape, and I sat at my desk. I remembered so much whispering about me and who my father was. When Brenda turned out to be pregnant, Grandma Mattie, Grannie Gran, Liza, Bertha, Marie, and all the elder women of the family met at Grannie's house to discuss the situation. Everyone had a different opinion on what to do about it. Brenda said she said that she didn't want a baby. Grannie Gran was against abortions and afraid that it could hurt Brenda. Adoption was out of the question.

The next problem. What were they going to tell the child when the child asked questions? Mom said she just "sat there minding her own business." She can't remember who said it, but they said this is going to be the mess that comes back.

Before her pregnancy, Brenda had a boyfriend, Rob Lee, a short, very dark man who lived across the street, but after the rape she hid from him. He came to the house one day, and she hid behind the couch. Grannie Gran let him in, and he told Brenda to come out of hiding from there and take a walk with him. While they were walking, his grandma yelled from her porch, "What are you doin' with that old pregnant girl? You goin' get yourself in trouble!"

He said shouted back, "This is my baby! We just kept it hid."

His grandma asked, "How'd you get that baby?"

He said, "The same way everyone else get babies." Brenda felt good that he stood up for her.

Mom told me that as I grew in her womb, she began to love me. On the day I was born, Mom said *everybody* showed up at the hospital, all wanting to know one thing. "What does she look like? Who does she look like?"

My mom replied, "She looks like a baby!" She was still living at home with her mother on Maffitt Street. She described me as a "pretty yellow baby." Everyone was fussy over me. Grannie Gran insisted I have diaper service, an extravagant luxury in those days, and everyone had to wash their hands before they could hold me. There was no kissing me on my face. After all, I was the first grandbaby and Grannie was very protective about some things.

Over a period of time, Mom and Rob Lee became closer. She eventually married him and began to have more children. I was still living in St. Louis during the early years of their marriage, but I didn't live with them. I lived with Grannie Gran, Grandpa Ted Sr., and Grandma Bonner. I remember being moved around a lot, but I did go often to visit my mother. Once I was there when she got into an argument with Rob Lee about him not coming home. We were standing in front of a four-family flat, and I was holding my baby brother in my arms. They began tussling, and he began to strike her in the face. She fell to the ground, and all I could see was him standing over her, beating and swinging on her. She was yelling and fighting him back, but he was winning. He knocked some teeth out of her mouth, and she was bleeding. I clutched my brother as we watched in terror.

After that day, I developed a fear of big dark men. Even small dark men could strike fear into my heart, and only recently have I been able to understand why and allow the Lord heal me of this. I witnessed my mom in many conflicts with men, and in many compromising situations. She had a desperate need to please men, as she searched for acceptance and love. I recognize the influence of that spirit of rejection and neediness in myself. It's like a generational curse that has followed me and my children. I fight daily with that part of me, learning to understand the Lord's unconditional love for me, and learning not to take everything that happens to me as a rejection or an attack.

Although I lived in California, I continued to go back to St. Louis for visits in my early childhood. It was always the same at home: Mom had another new boyfriend, new place to live, but the same old drama. I remember mountains of dirty clothes with that mildew smell, bathrooms that were filled with brown stains, holes in the walls, and bathtubs with wet dirty clothes. Many times, there was no electricity, no running hot water, but there was always special foods like steak for the boyfriends. We kids ate hotdogs.

Even though it was a dramatically different lifestyle living with Marie, I was still so happy to see my family that those things didn't bother me. Kids learn to adapt to anything. Me and my siblings had a special bond as siblings, and Mom was more like a sister because she rarely set limits or acted like a parent.

I know that I was blessed to escape a lot of the violence and beatings that my brothers and sisters had to go through. I could come and go, and nobody touched or hurt me while I was there. Maybe they were afraid of Marie. As my teenage life developed, I no longer went back for visits.

The last time I went to St. Louis to do my research, after interviewing parts of my family including my mother, she stuck a letter into my appointment book and told me to read it later. I didn't read it until I got home. I attempted to read it once or twice after arriving home, but I couldn't face it. Maybe I still felt angry or frightened, overwhelmed by all the pain and suffering of my family. Eventually I was compelled to sit down and read my mother's testimony. I believe that it's not just for my eyes only, but for the eyes and hearts of everyone. (See In Praise Section at the end.)

I was at the brink of a nervous breakdown from my separation from my husband, bankruptcy, and health problems—including chronic pain. Not to mention my discovering more about my family than I had planned for! I began reading this self help book; it was difficult because I was being resistant to facing the truth about myself. I would throw it down after reading parts that I wasn't ready to accept as my reality. *Who does this author think she is?* After a few days I'd pick it up, read that same part again, and I would see me and break out into tears. Sometimes it's very difficult for me to accept who I am, where I've been, and where I'm going. Most of it has to do with doing what I want to do and not the purpose that I've been born into. I knew it was a confirmation that even though it took me so long to get there, I was exactly where I was supposed to be.

I dove into the book and couldn't stop reading. I now realized that I had to set new standards. And if I don't live by my own standards, neither will anyone else. The one thing that I've learned in this book is that *I am definitely the value in the valley.* I've finally learned to be loving and kind to myself. Therefore, I won't be looking for it outside myself. This keeps me from lacking or falling short of anything (other than Christ Jesus), or turning to inappropriate old ways of seeking love.

I never stopped to enjoy or appreciate my own successes, because the next trial was already beginning. When I would experience a success, I felt I did not get the kinds of responses that I thought I should get, so I felt unsupported and my victories unseen. I was ripping myself off! Now I am moving on. The word of the Lord says, "Trust in the Lord with all your heart and lean not on your own understanding" (Proverbs 3:5).

FAMILIES FROM ONE MEMBER TO ANOTHER

I was taking Jerri, at the age of fourteen, to the doctor for a physical exam. She was sitting on the table, and the doctor was asking routine questions, when suddenly she began to tell us that she had been molested when she was three. Her father and his bride had gone out of town to get married, and she was left with her father's wife's family. His wife's son, who was a grown man, and some of his friends, took her and his little cousin into the daycare area of the house. He began to molest her, and when she resisted, he took out a gun and held it to her head. She then did what she was told.

At that moment, my yesterday was in the room. My heart was beating like a drum. I didn't want to fall apart because she needed me, but I felt overwhelmed with guilt. I just held her and cried with her. I was angry, and I wanted to get even, not just for her but for me too! *How does one get even?* (I found out later that there are statutory limits on prosecuting sexual crimes that have been committed over seven years ago.) The doctor witnessed this heart-rending scene and tried to bring comfort with offers of counseling and suggesting we file a police report, which we later did together. If I had known that they couldn't prosecute, I would have never taken her through that police reporting. I was ready to deal with her father and the mother, as well as the son, but my daughter was ready to let it go. Later when she told her father, he said he didn't believe it.

She's learning now as a mother to deal with receiving and giving affection. It isn't easy for her. She is quick tempered and defensive. I'm glad that she's not angry with me because I wasn't able to protect her, just like I wasn't able to be protected. believe it or not I've had hidden anger toward the adults, particularly my own mother and grandmother, because I wasn't protected. That is a mother's job. I blame myself as well as her father. We were both absorbed in our drug addictions and other nonsense, busy fighting each other for custody, instead of cooperating with one another for the children. We were leading separate lives. Although she's an adult now, the side effects of what happened to her show up in her behavior toward men. I believe she still needs help, hopefully to face her past and know her value.

Since my mom Brenda has been visiting, I am really trying to look at our relationship. I am remembering how she used to rumble through my things and bring about strife. I always thought of her as sneaky and out to get me. I feel this is somehow mixed up with my resentment of her not raising me. Now I am breaking free of these old thoughts and feelings by just loving her. I'm not hiding anything around the house, and I'm not hiding my feelings. I want us to share a deep and meaningful love between us. Sometimes a girl just needs her mother. A mother's love is about trust, truth, awareness, and action when need be. I'm willing to be what I'm asking for. All things that are old, I'm willing to let go. I am happy that I woke up one morning a couple of months ago and told the Lord that I needed to see my mother. He opened the door instantly. I want to use this opportunity to fix whatever is not right between my mother and me.

I'm looking at things differently now, and I'm reacting differently than I used to. I like confiding in my mother. Her reaction or opinions is not the issue; being with her and having her to talk to and laugh with encourages me. My solution for whatever I thought she might take is to take her shopping to buy her what she needs or wants. This sets me free, and I'm not bound by what she might do. In fact, she brought presents for me—a beautiful pearl shell necklace and a coat I thought I'd never see again. (I had left it in St. Louis a year ago.)

Now that my mom's back home, I've taken the time to be still and reflect on her visit. It was pleasant and sometimes fun. When I'd come home from work we would go out for dinner or shopping or just watch a movie together. She'd tease me about falling asleep during the movie. I told her I get some of my best sleep in the movies. She loved reading the book I'm writing.

She read it in two days. She said, "We're going to Oprah!" I told her she and Lavita will have to stand backstage so they don't embarrass us. She begged me for more pages and said she could see how God was working in my life.

Often, though, it was uncomfortable and difficult for me to be around her, mostly because of her health. She has asthma, and her loud wheezing scares the heck out of me. Every breath she takes sounds like it's the last. She can barely walk a few steps before she has to sit down. Her knees hurt her all the time. She doesn't eat a lot anymore, but she's still a very heavy woman. I believe that it is the Prednisone for her asthma. She's been taking it since she was fifteen years old, and it's taken a toll. We had a really close call and had to call the ambulance one night when she couldn't breathe. I found out that she left her medicine in St. Louis, and she didn't tell anyone that she needed to take it twice a day. I was able to see that she really did need it to survive. Having gone through a lot of my own health issues, my anguish and confusion about her has been replaced by compassion.

She did in fact rumble through my things, but she didn't take anything. I was actually grateful. She turned up things that I thought I'd lost! When I came home and saw that my things had been reorganized, she looked at me innocently with her big eyes and told me, "I just do things like that." I know she didn't get a chance to mother me when I was a kid, so she gets pleasure out of mothering me now. When she folds my clothes and straightens up my stuff or says, "What's wrong with Mama's big baby?" I know she is mothering me. So instead of being irritated, I see it as being rewarded, and I accept my mother's love in how she offers it.

I've learned that the key to my wholeness is giving. I'm released from the pain of my guardedness and can now open my heart and use whatever I have as an offering of love. "All that is not given is lost." I'm trusting that there will be enough, because my storehouse is from the Lord.

The changes in me are affecting me as a daughter, a sister, a mother, and a grandmother, as well as those around me. The giving of myself and my time to others is ricocheting onto my daughters. I have found myself to be the center—that's a servant's role—being humble, willing, and eager to serve.

The other day I mentioned to Kara all the duties I had to do for my mother while she was here. The tasks were difficult and time consuming.

She looked at me and said, "Mom, do you want me to do that for you?" It was a new moment in our relationship. I was aware that she wanted to take care of me, and now was able. That is a rewarding feeling! Even though I'm able to take care of myself right now, practice will prepare them for what may come later.

I needed nineteen t-shirts in various sizes to send back with my mother for the family in St. Louis. Later while I was at work, Kara took her baby and went to Walgreen's to get the California t-shirts. When I got home I went into the bedroom to help my mom pack. We went through the shirts Kara had bought, and every single one was perfect. She told me Kara had sat on the floor at Walgreen's with the baby in the car seat and made a mess picking the right shirts for everyone. She even got an extra one for my mom without being asked. Her labor of love did not go unnoticed, and I went into the living room and hugged her and thanked her for doing such a wonderful job. My mothering has changed—for over twenty years I "fussed and fist!" Now I "hug and help!" I wish I had learned this a long time ago.

Over the last two generations, the women have outnumbered the men by far, three or four to one. I believe that God is pruning the family tree, so that healthy branches can sprout and flourish. One of those healthy branches is my son Jason. I am proud to call him my son. As I think back to when he was two years old, he would go into the prayer closet and call down the power of the Lord. Wherever we took him, he would gather with the men, even going up into the pulpit with the pastors. I wasn't sure until recently that he does have a special anointing on his life. He is definitely part of the promise.

It was a Friday night when I arrived home from choir practice to learn that my son Jason had been summoned to Vallejo to his sister's house. His father, Jon, was in town. I immediately rushed to the phone to talk to my son. I was concerned about him. His father can be very tricky with mind games. I wanted to remind Jason that everywhere he went, the Lord Jesus was there too, and that I loved him. After talking to him, I was confident that he could handle himself in whatever situation was happening with his father's family. When I got off the phone, I turned to my daughters and I said, "Jon is going to be in church on Sunday."

Sunday was a rough day, I picked up my family for church. I was late for service, but I didn't want to miss church, because I was eager to get baptized. Unfortunately, that didn't happen. Just when I forgot that Jon was coming, I looked out the door and there he was. He looked older, dressed in a beige shiny suit with matching alligator shoes. I noticed he looked a bit worn. I turned my back and looked at my mother and said, "Mom, I told you he was coming." I felt him behind me, and he said, "Hi, how ya doin'? Where's my son?" I wanted to say, "*Where's my check?*" But the words wouldn't come out.

I turned around to be civil, and he introduced me to his wife whose name just happened to be the same as mine, LaWanda. I don't know how long it's been since I wore African attire, but both "new" LaWanda and I were wearing African attire. I felt like he'd found a replacement of me. The most beautiful and blessed part of the day was seeing his son Kawan who was at church too. I raised him, too, and his sister Marsha, too. He came to me to apologize for something he had done which offended me. It was a proud moment in a difficult day, because I saw the integrity in him that I never saw in his father.

PRAYER TRAVELS

History continues to repeat itself. Lavita's daughter, Rece, is fourteen years old. She is a thin pretty girl with big brown eyes. She was never raised by her mother, and she doesn't know the family. Like me, she was separated from her family. I believe if she got connected with us, it would bring out a closeness that she's not aware of yet. Recently she ran away from home, and nobody knew where she was. When she was spotted on the streets at night, her friends told the police she was involved in a lot of sex work and multiple partners.

I received a phone call from a detective in Chicago, who said that they had found Rece and that she had been in a shelter for the past two weeks. He said he didn't know what to do with her. They planned to go to court, and if they didn't hear from her family, they would make her a ward of the state. I was so overjoyed to hear that she was safe and sheltered, like we prayed. I ignored the negative things he said, and began to shout "Hallelujah!" right there at work.

I'd be willing to bet that Rece has a story, too. I asked the Lord to spare her and not let another generation suffer. She's still young, and with help and support from a loving family, she can make it. We can relate to her struggles—we've been there.

Before my trip to St. Louis, Aritha and I had talked on the phone about my abuse as a child by our uncle Kent, and by the end of the conversation, we were talking about *her* abuse as a child by our uncle (Ted Jr.). I was shocked to hear it, but I was still focused on looking into my own problems. I hadn't yet seen the connection between her, Auntie Cedra, and myself. I didn't know the extent of the problem in the family until I got to St. Louis and began to be flooded with stories.

I got a call from Nikki. She told me that she was going to escort Rece to California by bus. She didn't tell the child that she was moving her to California—we didn't want her to run. I wasn't expecting that, but I was looking forward to her visit. Nikki and I developed a deeper closeness since I took a trip to St. Louis. We talk every day by phone. I discovered myself watching her.

One morning I was laying in the bed, and I heard her having a conversation with Rece. What she was saying wasn't important, but it was her attitude, love, and directness. After she finished, she went back into the bathroom, and when she came out she burst out into crazy nursery rhymes—the same ones that I sing! I clicked a distant childhood memory of us singing together. We must have heard these songs when we were little, but as we were all torn apart, we used the nursery rhymes to remember our attachment to one another, because it was all we had! It seemed now to be our sisterly spiritual connection. We have carried these rhymes our whole lives. My kids were shocked. They had never met any of my siblings and to see someone act like me was strange for them! It brings me peace of mind and heart to know that I actually am not alone, not crazy, and I fit somewhere.

Nikki's time was getting short here, and we hadn't told Rece that she was staying. We asked her to walk with us to the store. I felt guilty because it was like I was being deceitful, but it was not my intention. On the way back from the store, she was holding her bag of candy and eating it, and I went up to her and hugged her.

I asked her, "How do you like California?" I didn't give her a chance to answer.

I said, "The Dingahs think it's best that you stay in California for four months until your mom gets out of jail."

She looked at me, took her forefinger to her mouth, and made a babyish bubbly sound. Then she asked, "Four months in California till my mother gets home?" And she just walked on down the street. There is something about her innocence, even after all she's been through; that moves me. It gives me a desire to be there for her. She has a good chance to be different. A few days later Nikki went back to St. Louis. Now after three weeks, her true colors have shown through. My idea was to build a solid and trusting relationship with her. I wanted her to become stable in her self-esteem and know her true value. I told her I was excited about getting to know her because I wanted to know who she was that God would answer my prayers about her. I didn't expect her to change overnight, but I'm glad that she's revealing herself, so I can get a better understanding of her and her mother. As Marie says, "You don't know you have a problem until you have arrived there."

Last night I allowed Rece to go out with a young man she knew before she came to California. She met him in Chicago when she lived there, so she said. He now lives in Oakland with his family. This was their second date. The first time his uncle came to meet us and pick her up. While I was talking to him in the house and looking at his driver's license and getting his phone number, my daughter Jerri went outside and wrote down his car's license number. Now mind you, I am the mother of four daughters, and I know the games. I'm a little rusty, but my daughters are now helping me do the screening. Normally I don't think that fourteen-year-olds are supposed to be dating, but Rece's circumstances were different. I wanted to see how far she would go if I gave her some room and responsibility.

It was around 10:20 p.m. when she left on her second date. She was supposed to be back by 11:30, but I thought it would be around 12:30. Perhaps I shouldn't have let her go, but even if I sent her to the store, if she was planning to run off, she will find a way.

By ten o'clock the next morning, she was not to be found, and a police report for a missing person had been filed. It's not exactly an Amber Alert, but we were concerned. We called the boy's uncle, and he said he didn't pick her up last night, and that she was not with the boy. My guess is she is with him or another boy. I should have checked the second time instead of trusting her too quickly. My bad. *I'm waiting for her to come back with my cell phone!*

My next question is: *What really happened to Rece and LaVita while in the custody of Bean?* They are so similar for not having lived together. They both seem to have a love-hate relationship with him, and with life. *What is my role to be in Rece's life?* I thought I would have her for at least four months and could make some kind of positive difference for her. The outcome is in God's hands, not mine. I had a difficult conversation with Rece. Looking in her eyes, I could see my own reflection. It was me as a little girl, Alice Lost Again. She's wandering in her own distorted world. It hurts me. I talk to her lovingly every day, but sometimes I have to use hard, cold facts and lay them on the table for her so she can visualize what's coming if she continues to do it her way. The lying and making up stories, cutting school, sneaking around with these Oakland heathens, and some other things we won't mention (family business), bring out flashbacks in my raising five daughters, where I would put my knee on their neck for such behavior. In fact, I did pin her down once, because I wanted her to know that I can get down and dirty if need be. Somehow, though, I know this is not what she needs. So we both have a lot more growing to do.

The flip side of this girl is she seems to be filled with such innocence. She is helpful, cleans the house, and gives me the most respect when she calls me "Auntie." I love her as I love my own daughters, and my feelings for her are growing. I want to have a positive impact on her. While we were talking, I wanted her to know that I see her clear as day, and I understand her. I told her I know something happened to her, because her reflection is too much like mine. If it wasn't molestation, it was probably violence or disappointment. It's time to get her some counseling, for whatever issues she might have. I told her, "Too bad we can't take a pill for this."

She replied, "Auntie, there ain't no pill for girls like us." In my heart I knew she was a true Dingette. I don't have much time with her, because her mother will be coming out of jail, and that's going to be a fight.

My heart is saddened. Rece has been missing for over a week. After three days I did file a police report. I know that I heard the spirit say, "Wait!" but feeling guilty I want to run out and start a search party. The real question is why am I feeling guilty? I guess because she ran away on my watch, after four months. What I expected to happen—that she would turn around her behavior and get rooted in the family and focused on her education—didn't happen. She got a phone call from her mama, and told her all about the whupping we gave her but not about all the love and support. The next morning when we dropped her off at the bus stop to go to school, she never came back. She called two days later and left a message, that she wasn't going to fool with us no more, and we wouldn't have to worry about her, because she wasn't coming back.

Although I had told her I would send her to her mother as soon as my credit card cleared, she chose not to wait. Did she really not want to go back to St. Louis? I can understand what that child is going through. She is so much like me and my sisters, but worse. At fourteen, she has the opportunity to express what's going on with her and get some help. She read parts of the book and heard our stories. Despite all this support to help her, she chose to connive and lie and run away, in order to stay covered, using sex and the internet as distractions from herself. She confessed to Jerri that she is doing what she wants to do with her life right now.

Finally, after three weeks of silence, we got a call from the San Mateo Police Department's Juvenile Division. They had found Rece listed on Craigslist under Sensual and Erotica. They explained that they randomly investigate websites that are covers for prostitution, and that Rece's ad had said, "New Girl in Town." She called herself Cookie and had posted pictures of herself spread eagled, asking men and women, "Why not treat yourself?" Her face looked very young, so the police called the number and made a date to meet Cookie. Shortly Cookie showed up at the arranged hotel with a female escort, twenty years old, who turned out to be her "pimp." The police solicited her for sex, she agreed, and they busted her for prostitution. She gave them false information, but eventually they matched her with the missing person's report that I had filed. So it wasn't a mistake after all.

My family and I were very disturbed and ashamed, but we still love her. Besides, how can I judge her when I've done as much or more? We are hoping that now she will get some help. However, it doesn't appear likely, because her mama is demanding that she be sent back to St. Louis. I was called to court on her behalf. There were many things I wanted to say to the judge, but for some reason the Lord didn't let me say it. I had an opportunity to talk to several probation officers and express my concern about her continuous rebellious and dangerous behavior. The crime carries a sentence of six months; however, if she stood up and admitted guilty to prostitution, they were going to waive the six months and return her to her mother in St. Louis. I know this is not the answer to the problem. She should have done the six months and gotten psychological evaluation and counseling.

When they called her name, the bailiff came out and got me as they brought her in from the holding cell. I looked at her, and she looked at me as if she didn't know me. I wondered what I was doing there, but when she stood up and admitted her guilt, I knew. I was there to witness that it was real, it did happen, and that it's not over. It appears that this time we all blew it, including her. But we don't know yet what God has planned for her. Remember we started praying for this kid a long time ago, and He dropped her on our doorstep for a reason. We'll just keep praying.

I got to see that there is so much work to be done in our family relationships. Talking to my sister LaVita (Rece's mom) in St. Louis was disastrous. She was full of ignorance and anger, and nothing got solved. She said the most awful things, called me names, and cursed me for interfering, but I had to remind her that she was the one who left her child out there alone while she was in prison. Furthermore, if she said her father did terrible things to her, maybe she didn't fight hard enough to protect her child from him. That sounds harsh, but it is the truth. The two of them are so much alike, even though they have hardly been together in fourteen years.

Another piece of the family puzzle fell into place yesterday. I had been so concerned about my youngest daughter's Deena's choices in relationships.

She had come home from court, where she got custody papers for her son, and we were driving over to get him at his father's house. The sheriff was going to meet us there.

She was quiet, and then she said, "Mom, I have to call Morgan and act like I'm still mad and not give him a clue that I'm on my way there." So she did, and her first words were, "Morgan, I want to see my son."

He began to tell her how much he loved her, using their son to lure her in. Even though he beats her up, spits on her, cheats on her, he still thinks he's taking care of her. I could hear the hurt in her voice, as she began to talk to her baby on the phone. I felt that a lot when my kids were taken from me by their father. It is so painful to see history repeat itself.

She told him she was on the way to her job, so he wouldn't get suspicious and leave with the baby. When she hung up, I looked at her and said, "Is this what you've been dealing with? I'll kill him myself!" I often have these thoughts, but of course, I can't act on them.

When we arrived, the police was waiting for us in their car. Deena started to panic when she saw that Morgan's car wasn't there. The door was open. The officer knocked, and they went in. I was relieved when I heard Morgan's voice and my grandson screaming when he saw his mama. I began to thank God. Somewhere inside, I have to hide the pain and anguish of raising children. I can't say everything I want to say, because it runs them away, even though it's the truth. So I lean on prayer and know that God is in control.

As we drove off with the baby, I could hear Morgan yelling that he was being threatened by our family. I had to laugh. On the way home, I began to tell her the reason I took Jason from his father was his abusive behavior. I didn't want my son to see a grown man beating on a woman, because I thought it would influence him to beat women. I told her, "If your son sees it he will repeat it." I became angry, remembering when the kids who lived with Lou and Jerri told me that he had beat Deena up so badly. I told Deena that I believe when a father treats his daughter like that he is giving her a signal that it is all right for other men to do you like that. He took my children away from me not because he wanted to raise them but to hurt me. They ended up getting hurt—one was molested and the other one became a victim of domestic violence.

At this point Deena said, "Mom, I got something to tell you. I've never told anybody but Morgan. When I lived in Michigan with my dad's family something happened to me too. Jerri doesn't know, because it would tear her apart. I'm all right with it. I just lived through it."

I felt like the walls were closing in, but I finally had my answer to why Deena couldn't love me freely. There has always been a wall between us, but I keep reaching through it. All I could think about was Nikki's story.

Where is my mother? I could hear all of our voices crying out for the protection of our mother that never came. It set up a root of bitterness.

I reached over and held her hand and kissed her head and told her I was sorry that I wasn't there and that I loved her, and that I'd known something was wrong. I sensed that something had happened to her, because her behavior showed it. And then I asked her, "What is it I can do for the wall to come down between us? I am willing to work on it." And she said she was too. It was a new beginning for us.

The Lord is so awesome. Deena and I are starting to form something new and real together. I understand her so much more since we had our little talk in the car. I'm able to accept her behavior because I recognize it myself earlier in my youth. I acted the same way because I didn't know how to express the things that happened to me, so instead I acted out, just as she's doing. It's not necessarily bad or taboo, but it's not constructive either. It's just struggling along, finding your way. I see she's driven to be a good mother, keeping her academics up and working twelve-hour days. She is a half year away from graduating from UCB. She says she wants to be able to educate her son and have a home for him. I'm proud because I can see that one generation has grown past me. She's also stood up for herself to a boyfriend who was disrespectful, and even though he said he was sorry, she had the character and courage to say, "I just left a four-year relationship of I'm sorries, and I don't intend to start another one." *Now that is growth.*

This is an important stage in my life as a parent, particularly with my daughters. I don't have to work so hard with them. I can just relax and receive the fruits of my labors, and all mothers know about that. If my kids need me, I'm there, but I don't have to run behind them—their lives are their own. No more codependency.

My son, however, is a different matter. I got a great laugh when I arrived home yesterday. There was a check from the District Attorney's Office for child support for my son. A little late. In fact, it's the second one in eighteen years. I really want to express my appreciation for the $12.95. I went from broke to rich! It gave me the opportunity to think about the space that my son and I are in, and what messages I am sending to him. We're at odds at the moment, but I trust that the Lord is working it out.

My son is wrapped up in his activities, which are very positive: mascot for Team Thunder for the Golden State Warriors, dance performances, journalism for the Post. He has done a lot of traveling and met a lot of important people who think highly of him and see his potential. On the other hand, as the only adult male in our family, his role is very important, and it's not about the smoke and flash of his celebrity status. He must find his place and purpose not only in the family but also in the world, and that involves getting educated and being responsible financially. He has a duty to become a male head in our family. He's eighteen and not a child anymore. I don't want to get in his way and delay his growth by continuing to baby him and pay his bills, when he can do it himself. Yes, it is pressure on him, but my job is to guide and direct him toward his calling. If a man doesn't learn to be responsible from his family, he'll never get it. I'm proud to say he's on his own and gave his life to the Lord so he gets it.

Recently I've had to face certain facts—that I am not in control of how people in the family will react to my story about our family secrets. I do however have to control how I let it affect me. The truth is unfolding and some pieces of this story are more ugly than nice. More and more I'm feeling the heaviness and pressure of what I must do. It's taken me twenty years to write the book, and there's nothing glamorous about it. It's slow and difficult work, partly because I'm just "waking up." I think people are glad I stayed asleep so long, especially the older people in the family (older than me) but not the Dingahs. I began the process, but others are being forced into it, and either they are going to deal with the truth, or they'll be swallowed up in their own bitterness and silence. I want to apologize for causing pain, but if it's any consolation, I'm in pain too, and I know it's necessary for our growth.

I've been thinking a lot about Aritha's (Dingah 2) daughter, Paula, who lives in St. Louis with her mother and her two sons. She's around twenty-five and has beautiful dark skin without a blemish. Her smile is filled with gorgeous large dimples and a gold tooth in the front. She has an inviting personality, though sometimes she gets very quiet. I observed how loving and gentle she was with her sons. Surely growing up watching her mother take care of her deranged family and deal with her own pain was very difficult for Paula. Her mother never really talked about what happened to her as a child, but she acted out strange rituals when Paula came in from a date. She would make her spread her legs and check her for sexual activity. The way her mom treated her seemed crazy to Paula because she didn't know why she was doing it. Unfortunately, mothers who have been sexually abused are often overbearing on the daughters, asking too many questions and probing into her personal business, but I know from experience it's just the mom trying to keep her daughter safe. I did the same thing in one form or another.

After Paula heard our testimonies, she was relieved to know that we just weren't totally crazy for no good reason. She told me how much she loved her mother and I knew it was true because I could see the beauty of her mother in her. This girl has a husband in the penitentiary, but she is faithful to him, committed to taking the kids to visit him, as well as taking care of his other daughter. Where I see us Dingahs in her is in her determination to make it work. That shows strength and courage. However, she limits herself by not driving or exploring new opportunities. Her sons are growing up and need long range supervision like all teenagers. We'll see how it works out for her someday. It's a long journey home to healing and deliverance.

ALICE IN WONDERLAND

I don't know where this book may lead, but doors will open and doors will shut. Every morning that I rise out of bed, I look in the mirror, and I don't always see that beautiful woman that others claim to see. I see the scars of my disobedience, stress and strain of having it my way, and a little frightened girl, Alice, who has come so far, and has further to go. Then I look again and I see a grownup woman, Alice, who is no longer wandering in Crackland. She has arrived in Wonderland (not to be confused with Wanderland!). To wander means to move about with no destination or purpose, to gallivant around in search of pleasure—just thoughtless, idle travel. For many years, I wandered in search of something that wasn't real, living in my imagination. Through God's grace I found my way to a marvelous and real place, where Truth lives; you could call it Wonderland. The Alice that lives there faces life with strength and courage and trust.

I am tired today of self-pity. Yes, I've been kicked, wounded, stompted—yes, stompted—and shafted, ridiculed, and dumped, but hey, I have a glorious future ahead of me. I know that I'm now at the point where I need to go and find the testimonies of the men in the family. This will not be easy. I am feeling intimidated, but I have no choice but to complete my mission. This is a job for Jarasta, who lives to stand in a fight. She may have fear but it's acted out in toughness and strength. She is the survivor!

I thought I wanted to start with Ted Jr. because he's the one I have a lot of compassion for, and I wasn't his victim. He has continued to go in and out of recovery programs for his drug and alcohol abuse. I wanted him to have time to get stable before I hit him with hard questions, but I realize now the timing doesn't matter. He's in and out, in and out, and there's never going to be the right time to talk to him. I've determined to carry my tape recorder and a blank cassette, and wherever I catch him, I do not care.

When I've shared the beginning of this story with other men, some of them have "come out" to me and talked about childhood incidences that I never expected. They are quick to talk about being abused themselves, but not one yet has said they were the abuser. A patient of mine, a blind man, was escorted to my office by his caretaker, and somehow we got on the subject of my book. As I began to share about my being molested, tears began to roll down his face. He broke down and started sharing with me how he was molested by his priest in church. The priest told him that if he told anybody he would go to hell. The man started sobbing, clutching the big silver cross he was wearing, and screaming in a high-pitched voice, "But I love God, I love God." I grabbed a hold of his hand and told him that the guilt and shame was not his. He asked me how I got over my pain. I told him that I allowed God to come in and wash me clean. The world is a crazy place, bad things happen to good people, good things happen to bad people, but you have to live for today, letting go of the past. He said, "Bless you!" and began to pray for me. I am hoping that some of the men in my family and others who read this will feel free to tell the truth, because they know, it's not about judgment of them, it's about truth and healing.

WHAT YOU LAY IN VEGAS WON'T STAY IN VEGAS

My trip to Vegas was more extraordinary than I could have ever imagined. I had an intention of leaving God at the airport, and picking Him up on my way back home. If you could only have seen me, you wouldn't have known the Christ in me. Willfully seductive, on the prowl, and tired of no intimacy, it has never been in my experience not to feel the touch of a man. In Vegas, I arrived at Angel's wedding in appropriate attire and very high heels. The reception was where it all began to unfold. My cousin offered me a glass of wine, and that turned into three. Hey, we were celebrating. By the way, this is the same cousin that Aritha claims she had consensual sex with as a child. I took my tape recorder, but the music was too loud for me to use it, so I had to rely on my ability of listening. Some of the words might be turned around, but I did capture my cousin's response. It's amazing how bold a few drinks can make you.

I started with asking him if he'd heard about my book, and he said no. Then I explained about how I was molested as a child, and this led me to researching the family history and uncovering other women's stories about their abuse. I then asked him if he remembered Aritha. He said, "Yes, ain't that your sister?"

I said, "Yes. She told me that you and her used to have consensual sex when you were kids. She said you didn't force her, that she was willing."

He immediately denied that it was him. "She must have me mixed up with one of my other brothers. I had no mama, and I had just lost my daddy. I wasn't thinking about nothing like that. I was full of anger and bitterness."

I thought that was a nice neat answer, so I asked him another question. "Why would you think something like that would happen, where men in the family would be touching the girls?"

His response was, "There was no male role models, having to raise yourself." He used a lot of words to justify it, but he still insisted that it wasn't him. I asked him later on if I could call him and set up another interview, and he agreed.

The after party was at the Luxor Hotel. Never have I seen such a gorgeous bridal suite! Rose petals everywhere, lit candles all around the Jacuzzi, and everything made for two. No more Howard Johnson's for me! Of course, the bride wasn't at her party—she was out gambling. So Lola, Bebe, and I went downstairs to gamble too. I won a hundred dollars and put it in my purse and got up and left. I'm not a gambler; I need a prize to come out of the machine that I can take home. So, Bebe dropped me and my high heels off back at Howard Johnson's, and I told myself that there's always tomorrow.

The next day I got up and went shopping on the strip. I got a couple of free passes to some clubs. I don't really club, but I was in Vegas. I decided to take a chance and go out. I went to the Coyote Ugly Club, where patrons, mostly women, get up on the bar and dance. It's encouraged by the dancers who work there, who pour the women shots from the bottle straight into their mouths. That's to get them loose. I came there loose. I wanted to do one thing— dance on that bar. After a double shot of a Cadillac, I was standing next to some girl, telling her to go ahead and get a shot. Then I looked to my left and saw a cute white boy, a Marine. When I told him I was thinking of dancing on the bar he said, "Do it, girl, I'll be right here waiting for you." I had all the willpower and false courage I needed, so I headed toward the bar, shakin' it. Now I know why Christians don't drink.

One of the bouncers helped me up, and I was all up there by myself. Actually, it was Chickie up there, having a ball. Before I knew it, all the other big girls were up there with me. I think I started a trend in Coyote Ugly. Big girls shake it up, and the boys roar. Later, I tried to pick up the Marine, but when we got to the hotel, things just wouldn't stand up. I didn't know what the reason was, but I was already planning my exit. And yes, I did at least get something from him—cab fare. In Vegas, cab fare's expensive.

You would think that was the end of my evening, but oh no. I left the hotel carrying a big Vegas-sized cup of Cadillacs. I decided to use my other club pass. The other club was at the far end of the strip. I was drinking so much I was floating, but at least I changed my shoes into fancy flip-flops. On the way I met another young guy who was standing at one of the hotels passing out his CDs. Chickie sized him up and figured surely he could do the trick. I took his CD and his number and told him I'd call him after midnight. When I got to the other club, I had a great time talking and dancing. I met an African guy I thought about hooking up with, but when he turned his back, I was gone. I had to walk back...in fact, I can't remember exactly how I got back to the hotel. I called the guy with the CDs and told him where I was, and he said he was coming over. I woke up in my red negligee, alone in my room. I don't think my company ever arrived, and if he did, I don't think I answered the door.

The lesson I learned from this trip was about validation. I thought that I had left the Lord at the airport, but as my sober mind reflects back, He was there all the time to derail Chickie's plans for the Great Vegas Getaway. In fact when I got home, I called my pastor, not to confess but to ask about the singles' class. I started telling him about my trip, and that I was feeling very disturbed and disappointed in myself for willfully trying to commit sin. I didn't find much pleasure in it, and it didn't hold the same kind of value that it used to for me. It's not what I want to do. I have a real desire in my heart to live saved and live for Jesus. It's this flesh that drives me crazy. Everything that I shared with Pastor he responded to with encouragement. I joked, "You just have an answer for everything!"

We said our goodbyes and hung up. I was in shock that I had just confessed everything to the pastor, and he was so accepting, but that's his nature. I called him the next day and left a message on his voicemail, apologizing for anything disrespectful I might have said, and that I loved him as my pastor and father.

In the meantime, my convictions were weighing heavy on me, not so much because of sin, but the idea that my flesh can appease me, but it's not pleasing. The validation lies within myself. I keep looking for it in people, places, actions, and things, but I'm disappointed every time. I need to exercise my faith that God alone validates me. I have learned my self-worth lies in me.

What am I bringing to the table and offering other than sex? Sex is a wonderful thing but it has its proper place and time. For me, sex in the beginning of a relationship is inappropriate. It is the wrong foundation and it leads to false intimacy and a house full of children. You can lay on your back forever and all you'll get is bedsores and babies.

When I got home, I thought about Cousin Dante's answers to my interview questions at the wedding. I informed Aritha later that she would have to give me more details if I was going to get to the truth. After numerous attempts, I was finally able to get more details from her. She said it definitely was Dante. I asked her where these events had taken place. On Maffitt Street, under the porch steps, or in the back room…was her response.

I shouted, "Oh my God. A wicked house! Thank the Lord it's no longer there." So I asked, "How did this occur?"

She said, "Wanda, don't you remember how we used to play house? You know you need a mama and a daddy. I had already been exposed to sex with Ted Jr., so this was just somebody of my choice. It didn't matter if it was my family …"

I asked her who initiated it. She said she couldn't remember, but it was probably her. She liked him.

She started laughing when she recalled that one day when they were at his house and the family was supposed to go somewhere, but Uncle Harry wasn't ready. So the two of them snuck into the back and got into Uncle Harry's blue truck. She said they was on the floor doing it. They were scared they might get caught, but it didn't stop them. That wasn't shocking to me, but her next sentence was.

She said, "Wanda, don't you remember the blue truck? It's the same truck they took you to the train station in when you left for California." I drew a blank. More and more as these blanks happen to me, the more I want to live in the glimpses of safety of those visions of heaven. I don't want to live my life in pieces and parts. Since I don't remember, I just live with what I do remember—the good and the bad. I remembered the old car parked in the back yard, but I never remembered the truck.

Later I found out that it really wasn't cousin Dante, but one of his brothers. So the man was being truthful, and I was relieved because I grew up with him and never felt that spirit around him.

GIVING FREELY

A few weeks ago, it was a Saturday morning and I got up and picked up some flowers and headed over to the dialysis center to see Grannie Gran. She was asleep in the recliner while she was having her treatment. I stood there for a while, deciding whether to wake her. I watched how frail and old she looked, with her dark brown skin all wrinkled, no teeth in her mouth, and her body had begun to shrink and wither. She was disappearing right in front of my eyes. I knew that these were her last days. I really wanted to know what kept her going, and why.

I gently shook her and greeted her with a big smile and the flowers. It took her a couple of minutes, but I saw my face register in her mind. I pulled up a chair and sat beside her. I'm always cautious now about mentioning my book. Although it's one of the most exciting things in my life, I'm afraid to share it with her, because I saw her fear during our testimonies in St. Louis. I had given up a long time ago interviewing my grandmother. Something was different about her this visit.

She seemed open and wanted to talk. I never knew her daddy's name was Ezekiel Simmons, and he became a preacher after getting struck by lightning. She said he used to be a "cussah," cussing up a storm. One day he was in the yard, cussing and drinking, and a storm came up. Lightning struck his suspenders, and from that day forward he became a praiser. She remembered him coming into her room when she was a young woman, and telling her, "Me and your mama ain't gon' make it. I'll see you around."

She said it was a long time before she saw him again, and when she did, he had remarried another woman, who was "an ugly woman." In the meantime, her mother, Grandma Mattie, had also married again. Grannie said his name was Papa Ford. He walked with a limp, so her and Marie called him "Hopping Ford," and they both liked him. Grannie Gran had to see the puzzlement on my face because she said, "I know it's confusing, but I also married a man whose last name was Ford, but no relation."

I was so excited that she had opened up to me, I couldn't wait to run home and call Marie and tell her about our breakthrough. I'm trying to spend quality time with Grannie, but I do think she's afraid to be around me for long periods of time. I did get her the day after Thanksgiving and brought her to my house. After an hour, she was ready to go home. I said, "Ready to go home so soon?"

She said, "I been here over an hour!"

The holidays are here, and I'm so ready to be jolly. I want to put the immediate past behind me—at least until I finish the book. I'm starting to see the light of day about who I am, and I'm not crying so much. I've learned a lot about me this last couple of years. Even though it's been hardships and painful moments, especially around the breakup of my marriage, God has a plan and I have a purpose. So often I have looked across the room and seen someone else's life that looked so good from that distance, and I asked, "What the hell's wrong with me?"

I want you to know that I have figured out that there is not a darn thing wrong with me. My life is not my own, therefore a lot of things I would choose to do with it I can't do, nor do I want to do any more. I've been listening to testimonies about other women who simply just stopped willful sin and were blessed. It's called sacrifice, surrender, and obedience. I'm ready to give my whole heart to the Father without leaving one of my hands behind my back. I know that no matter what I go through from this day forth, He is in the midst. My portion of life, love, and liberty is in the basket.

Folks, the Lord has given me bountiful gifts and a host of new beginnings, over and over. The Bible says the Lord takes care of babies and fools (Psalms 107:17). Well, I'm both! But I'm okay with that. What I see in my Father, I want to see in my husband, otherwise what's the point? I've gotten too old to concentrate on someone just bouncing up and down on me. My passions have changed from earthly things to things more spiritual. I'm still made of flesh, and when I see a good-looking guy and he smells good, the pistols start firing. If he goes right, today I will go left. To insure that I don't get crazy when I'm around men, I've ordered a bottle of men's Mesmerize cologne (buy one, get one free). At night I spray it all over my pillows. My pillows have names: Mark, Matthew, Luke, and John. Peter and Paul lay on the floor, and I flip them boys all night long. They smell so good, and I cling to them. I trust that the Lord knows my needs, and if I don't get in the way, He won't delay.

I couldn't put it off any longer. I needed a Christmas tree. I left my house blindly as I so often do, without a clue as to how to get a large tree home by myself. This is impulsive behavior, for which I am famous. At least this time it's not about a man, drugs, or expensive jewelry—it's about making a special Christmas for the kids. We have two new babies this year! I had a short amount of time to do it, since I was meeting Julie later to go with her to her chemo treatment.

Off to Home Depot I went, very excited. When I stepped into the huge lot, there were trees everywhere. I didn't want to be too cheap, but I didn't want to be too expensive, so what should I do? A worker came to help me. We picked a standard tree, around seven feet tall. He told me he could put it on top of the car but I would have to tie it on. Store policy. I told him I was a soldier and I was going to get that tree home. He showed me where the twine was, and I was feeling optimistic.

But then it happened. I heard a man's voice shouting, "I had a wife when I came here. Where is she?" Every emotion I could possibly have came flooding in. What am I doing buying a Christmas tree alone? My husband always got the trees, brought them home, and put them up, for the past eight years. I felt lost, confused, sad, abandoned, and my tears fell like raindrops.

What I realized though, is yes, I still had anger issues around the breakup of my marriage, but I was filled with courage and determination that I was going to accomplish my task without a husband. I tied it on top of the car and I called Deena for help getting it in the house, and together we did it. My depression melted as we struggled and stumbled to get it through the door, laughing like fools. It was a precious moment with her!

We set it up in the living room, and I stared at the tree for two days, wanting to decorate it, but I wasn't quite ready. After the second day, I decided to move on it. I gathered up the grandchildren, and we poured eggnog, turned on the Christmas CD, and we began to jump and dance and decorate. I want to leave a loving impression on them, to be free with them like I wasn't able to be with my own children when they were little. When dealing with the responsibility of providing for your family, you can forget to stop and just enjoy them and the moment. There's no real manual about raising children. If there is, it wasn't in the ghetto where I was. There's just guesses. And I guess I've learned something: just relax and enjoy.

The tree was beautiful. It had presents under it, and ornaments with the grandkids' names on them. It had candy canes, snow, tinsel, and colorful lights. It was a total fantasy Christmas tree, and it washed away the old and brought in the new.

There was love in the air. Everywhere I went I saw people

kissing and hugging, and I wasn't mad. I've always been a hopeless romantic, and thank God, I'm not tainted by disappointment. I'm learning more about me as a woman every day. The biggest thing I learned was I never allowed healing in any broken relationships with men. I just moved on, since the age of sixteen years old, trying to hide my feelings. However, I was still carrying the weight of those sad feelings, and how awful some of those men treated me. I realize now though that a lot of it was my own fault. It's about choice. If you cast your pearls before swine, they're still pigs, and you're still going to end up muddy.

Riding in my new 2005 Ford Taurus, I headed to work in San Francisco. I kept taking the wrong turns. I felt like I was exploring new territory, or old territory with new eyes. It had something to do with the newness of the car—it seemed to have its own cruise control. For some reason, I began to think of Mr. Randall, Marie's old boyfriend, the mechanic. He taught me to drive. My driving record is impeccable because of his training. I had forgotten what a kind and gentle soul he seemed to me as a child, a man whose interest in me was healthy. For a moment, I missed him, and remembered how much he meant to me as a child. Over the years I've run into him, but it's always been in passing. I didn't know what really happened between him and Marie. I just knew that one day he was gone. I blamed myself, as well as Marie, for running him away, but I got over it, or at least forgot it.

I value the relationships I have with men where there is no physical intimacy because the love is free, like with Mr. Randall. He just poured training, love, and skills into me. I remember the joy of being a little girl with him as my father figure. Marie always had a way of smoothing over the rough and painful edges. She worked her MSW magic and things fell into place.

This brings me back to Rece. I hoped I could help smoothe some edges for her. I thought about all the hardships in my relationships, so when I found some letters and notes in the things she left I was connected with her. I could feel all her pain and know the road she's headed down—I've been there. One letter to herself in particular represents the inner child Alice crying out. It's called, "Why did I?" She talks about her relationship with a guy and how painful it is, yet how she is driven uncontrollably to be there with him. It says:

"I dealt with that for three years. Why I don't know. The beatings, the torture, the pain, the feeling of not being loved, or is this the way he shows me he cares? It's not fair how I fall to my knees begging him please. How I'll do anything, give anything for him, because I love him. How do you love such a beast? It makes no sense. All the pain lying in a hospital bed, on the verge of death, but I pulled through just to go through it again and again. But the more I was in the hospital, the more tired I got and I just couldn't take no more. I walked out the door ..."

This letter reflects both her weakness and her strength, and the weakness and strength of all the women in our family. We are survivors who have endured the worst. It is my belief that we can come out and be whole. I know that love covers a multitude of sins, so right now I want to put the covering of protection and the Lord's salvation over her and her mother. The only way I know to do that is through prayer, so that's what I'm doing.

Rece is missing again. Last seen in St. Louis, living with her mother, and going out on a date with a twenty-two-year-old who somehow passed her on to a twenty-eight-year-old. She is now fifteen. The family is worried because this guy is supposedly a dangerous man—rumor has it that he has killed someone. His own father was out looking for him when he found out the girl was only fifteen. The whole thing just makes me sick to my stomach, not out of judgment, but out of compassion. I see myself in her, me in the next generation, with circumstances that are more profound. I trust the

Lord to make a way. This is where I learn to exhale. We just found out that she is going to have a baby. God has a plan.

There was a homegoing in the family on Monday. Parts of me were afraid to show up, worried about rejection from members of the family who would be there. Not everybody is happy about the book. Guess what, sometimes I'm not happy about it either. I took two of my daughters and their kids with me for support. It's nothing like new life that brings togetherness. It was Auntie Jo's son Laymon who passed, only thirty-three years old. He'd had a bad heart all his life.

I hugged and kissed everybody, and it felt so good to be accepted and loved in the family.

Now the truth about who God is in my life happened at the reception. I heard the Lord tell me to go over and hug Auntie Cedra, and I got up and walked straight out the door. I was intercepted by another aunt who had suffered, along with her children, much more than I ever had from the cruelty of rejection because she was Ted Jr.'s ex-wife. She encouraged me to do what God told me to do. It was like a fire was lit under me then. So I boldly went over to Auntie Cedra, who was having a conversation and ignoring me. I waited patiently for her to acknowledge me. She looked up, and I bent down and threw my arms around her and squeezed her and kissed her cheek. Then I said, "I love you, Auntie." I didn't directly look in her face or wait for her to give me a response. She just chuckled, and I went on my way.

On Valentine's Day, I was on my way out the door, when my daughter informed me that it was Valentine's Day. I don't know how it slipped up on me. It is normally my favorite holiday. I yelled, "No, it's not!" I got stuck for fifteen minutes in the house, tripping on the fact that it was also my anniversary date. I had a rough day at work, and of course I didn't hear from Vince. I grew up a little more this year. Ladies, if somebody don't want you, they don't want you. "He's just not that into you." Get over it!

Actually, the Lord gave me Deuteronomy 8:6, which talks about the Promised Land and walking into a new life. He gave me an illustration using a picture of my old co-workers. I looked at it and realized I missed them. The question came to me: Do you want to go back? I said *no*. Then the answer came—if you only knew what was ahead, you would never want to go back. It's a metaphor for my marriage. It has nothing to do with either my or Vince's unrighteousness; it has to do only with the Lord's righteousness. He brings about separation in its right time. I did have a good evening. Deena took me out for dinner and jazz. She chose to spend Valentine's Day with her mama, not her boyfriends.

It's time to schedule that vacation time to St. Louis. I'm ready for the next step of the book. Perhaps open a few doors for the men in the family. They have been dealing with alcoholism and drug addiction, hiding from the past. Brothers, let's all be free.

At work, I've been given a promotion. I have more responsibility than before. I'm really just a clerk, but I'm actually in charge of running the new San Francisco branch of the Medical Marijuana Program for the state of California. Sometimes we think our job is mediocre, but the Bible tells us not to despise small beginnings. Any job that God gives you, do your best. You never know where it will lead you. People on my job say that I am so tough. At first I felt insulted, but the more I work this position, I know that toughness is required, as well as fairness and compassion. The job and I go together well.

FACE TO FACE

I saw Ted Jr. last night, only because my son Jason called to inconvenience me, asking me to take his friend back to Oakland at 11 p.m. I was just finishing getting my hair done, and it was a bit out of the way, but after some persuasion and persistence by Jason, I agreed. I headed toward downtown, as always keeping an eye out to spot Ted Jr., and suddenly, there he was! I pulled over and screamed out his name. I was so excited that after six months he had appeared.

When he saw me he first dropped his head, but then he came on over. I tried not to notice his appearance—he looked like he'd been wearing the same dirty clothes for a long time—but I just wanted to let him know that we miss him, and his mother wanted to see him. He asked me for two dollars, and I gave him five. We agreed that I would pick him up at 11 a.m. tomorrow the next day to take him to the dialysis clinic to see Grannie Gran. We said our goodbyes; he walked away from the car, but then he turned and signaled me. He said, "It gets lonely out here sometimes. I miss and love you guys. I just needed to tell somebody that." For me that was a major breakthrough.

I was late getting started the next morning, and arrived twenty minutes late. Ted Jr. was nowhere to be found. I searched the Tenderloin streets for forty-five minutes, but he had disappeared. I pulled myself together and went to see Grannie. I debated whether or not to tell her I'd seen him, but I took a chance. She was relieved to hear that he wasn't dead. She said, "He's still my son. I love him. I want to see him. It's been four years."

I watched her face, and in her eyes, I could see a search for something familiar, some sense of control for her own life again. Even I know she's coming to the end. I told her I would keep looking for him, and in the meantime, we would ask God to take care of it for us. She smiled.

Kara had agreed to wash Grannie Gran's hair, so we picked her up one morning. The ride to Kara's house goes through the Tenderloin, and of course, I searched eagerly for a glimpse of Ted Jr., trying not to be obvious. There was no sign of him. I felt compelled to comfort Grannie somehow. Sometimes she looked so lost. She was in a lot of pain and often alone. I used my cell phone to call her sister Liza in St. Louis. Then we called Miles, who lives in Palo Alto. Grannie seemed to revive and began to talk about her day center for seniors, which a friend of mine owns. It keeps her going to have things to do between rounds of dialysis.

The following Saturday I went to visit Grannie again. I go more often now. She smiles when I walk through the door. There is even a chair waiting for me. It reminds me of me being a child, sick, with her sitting by *my* bedside. She was complaining of so much pain in her legs and her mouth. I began to pray for her, asking her to say, "Lord Jesus." She was looking all around to see who was watching or hearing. I didn't want to get distracted, so I closed my eyes. I prayed for her, asking God to forgive her and ease her pain. I asked that she would allow God to come into her heart. I could feel His presence upon us. I squeezed her hand. When I finished I opened my eyes and she had a look of fear on her face. I had felt it before in myself, and I've seen it in others, the resistance to surrendering when God comes.

She said, "I wish Marie was here. She can just lay her hands on me and I feel better."

I told her in return that I am a praiser and a worshipper, not a healer. She laughed and said, "That's good too."

Indeed people were watching and listening, but it didn't matter. I'm not ashamed of the Gospel.

I had been visiting Grannie for several months when one slow morning at work, Ted Jr. peeked over my partition. I was shocked. When you least expect something, there it is. He came in and sat down, and soon he had nodded off. I let him sleep while I worked, then asked my boss if I could take an early lunch. I woke him up and asked, "Are you hungry?"

"Uh, huh," he said.

"Let's go to lunch," I said.

I told him I needed to make a stop first. My phone rang, and a friend asked where I was. Before I thought, I said, "I'm going to visit my Grannie at dialysis."

Ted Jr. said, "What?"

I just smiled. He actually looked presentable that day and didn't smell as bad as the last time.

When we arrived, Grannie was laying there asleep. I told him to go and wake her up. You had to be there to witness the look on her face. Such joy to see him, and him to see her. He laid his head on her bosom like a small child, and she began to stroke his back, mothering him. All I could do was thank God. It was an amazing moment.

After we visited, it was lunchtime. We went to a Mexican restaurant and sat down to eat. I began asking him questions.

"What is your name on the streets?"

He said, "Saint Louis, or Ponytail."

I asked him how he was surviving out here. He told me he was stealing and hustling, and he stayed with different people, using crack or food for a place to crash. He said he had no peaceful sleep. Sometimes he said he stays up for six or seven days straight, and then he falls into a coma and wakes up robbed. *What a miserable life,* I thought, remembering my own past.

He began to talk about Auntie Cedra, saying how close they had been when they were little. In fact, she has a knife wound on her chest because someone came looking for him and stabbed her instead. They were teenagers at the time, flirting with death. He opened the door to his and Auntie Cedra's relationship, and I was ready to walk through it.

"So what happened between you and her?" I asked.

He said, "Sometimes I would sit across the street from her house crying. I wanted to ring the doorbell, but every time I tried to talk to her she wouldn't talk to me."

I said, "But what really happened between you?"

He replied, "I don't know if she knew it or not, but Gill (her husband) and I used to get high together. We were in the basement and I asked him to loan me some money, and he wouldn't. I got upset because I loaned him money when he asked. I felt he was obligated to me. When he didn't, I snatched some stuff off the wall and ran."

"But what happened to you and Auntie Cedra before that? When you were little?"

"What did you hear?" he asked.

I said, "She told me you molested her."

He said, "I did some crazy things, but I didn't do that."

I went on to tell him that I had the testimony of at least two more women in the family that said he molested them. I said, "They all told me that when the newscaster, Robin Williams, came on at ten, you would tip into their rooms and pull them out to do sexual acts with you. Neither one of these women knew about the other, but their stories coincide."

Ted Jr. fidgeted a bit, trying to have a stern face. It reminded me of the same look Grannie gave me when I told her Kent was molesting me. It was such a look of cold denial. He looked so much like Grannie at that moment. I didn't know if he would admit that he had done such things, but it really didn't matter whether he did or not. Confronting him was the important thing. I had given him a chance to tell his story, but he didn't take it.

I went on to tell him that until you can face yourself and admit to yourself what you did, you would be lost. Forgiveness comes from God. If you ask Him to forgive you, it doesn't matter whether a person forgives you—that's on them. I searched his face for an encouraging sign, but there was none. We finished our meal and I told him that if he ever wanted to talk to me, he knows where I am.

It always seems that whenever I travel some natural or personal disaster always happens. My trip to St. Louis was scheduled a week before they had a blackout from the rainstorm. The city was without electricity, but I cut off the news and said, "The Lord knows I need to get to St. Louis. When I get there, there will be power. I can't do what I need to do in the dark!" And it happened.

Jody and I arrived that evening, picked up the rental car, and headed to Mama's (Brenda's) house. We got Mama and went to Nikki's house. I was excited to see everybody, but inside I was filled with fear. I was focused on doing a job, getting testimonies for the book. Everywhere I went I carried a tape recorder, pencil and pad, and a camera, just like a reporter. The Dingahs went with me on the interviews, providing much needed support. We moved as a united front. When we arrived, people would say, "Here come the Dingahs." Of course we were wearing our gold numbered Dingah T-shirts.

It was different this time. Last time we stumbled around, gathering information, but this time we used the information we already had to conduct detailed interviews. Our mission was to jolt people's memories about the life and times of 4014 Maffitt Street, and to gather their stories.

Our first interview happened by chance at Aritha's house. Grannie's youngest son, Ford, was there. Although his language is full of profanity and "N-words," he was upright and true to the game. He is always himself, never changing no matter who is around. People in the street fear and love him at the same time. As a child, I remember him taking apart any appliance and putting it back together again, usually. He works on cars, construction sites— you name it, he is gifted.

He does have about thirteen kids with at least three different women. He has six sons named after him.

We were all sitting in the living room visiting. Ford came in with a pack of beer and his son-in-law, Polo. After greetings, I asked him if he would consider doing an interview with me. He laughed and said, "I ain't got nothing to say."

So I turned to Polo and said, "Why do you hang out with Ford?"

He said, "I was messing with his daughter and people used to say, 'When Ford find out he gon' kill you.' But that didn't stop me, 'cause I really liked her. When I met Ford, I really liked him, too."

Ford busted in and said, "Polo, I like you, too. At first I didn't but now you my boy."

I asked Polo why it was that people fear and respect Ford. He said, "He be keeping it real. Whatever he says has a meaning to it. Like 'wake up!' He's a unique person. We been on jobs together, and I done made good money."

Ford said, "The boys in the street are wild and messed up. I don't know why these kids keep turnin' out like that. I admit I was ignorant in the past too."

With Ford, I persisted in having a casual conversation with his friend, hoping to learn more about Ford or hoping that Ford would open up. But Ford was guarded, even warning Polo to watch what he said and quit talking so much. However, Ford did comment on the many different last names of his siblings, bearing witness to Grannie Gran's history. The different names of the children is a significant piece of the puzzle. Many of us in the family are interested in how Grannie acquired the name Ford, since Ted Sr.'s mother's name was Bonner. As we recalled, Grannie's mother Mattie was married to Papa Ford, then Grannie told me she married Ted Sr. Ford, no relation. Very confusing. Ford had given me several phone numbers of male members of the family.

ALL CARDS ON THE TABLE

There is a card game they like to play called Tonk, and they don't use Monopoly money. I recall walking into the kitchen and seeing my sister Aritha and her husband Gene. They sat down at the table and began to play cards. I've never quite seen cards played like this between a couple. They were cutthroat, shouting crazy things like "Transvestite!" and "Broke heathen!"

As they began to lose money to each other, real hostility showed up. I felt a bit uncomfortable, but everybody else said it was normal. They even said it was like an aphrodisiac for them. Later on that night, the whole family was sitting at the table gambling. Sometimes they went on for two or three days! Children and adults! And nobody gives the money back. It's a family addiction and sickness, *and they all should go to therapy.*

I contacted Dale and his brother, Lucius Junior.

That afternoon we went to Dale's house first but he wasn't there, so we left a note with a number for him to call. Then we went to Lucius Junior's house. Ironically, he lived at the forty-second block of Maffitt Street. That was a laugh.

It had been so many years since I'd seen him. He had aged a lot, but I could still see that suave charm he always had about himself. He used to be a real sizzling dresser, but with age, he has slowed down. He works in a nursing home. He's been with the same woman, Martie, for eighteen years. They never married, and he declared he had no interest in getting married.

"For what?" he would ask.

He invited us into his bedroom where he was relaxing in a big chair. There was a fan blowing that had no cover, and it made me nervous since there were grandkids around. It brought up my mother instinct, but I didn't mention it. I just kept watch.

As I began to tell my story about my childhood on Maffitt Street and the book, Martie said, "Is there some stagg that goes with this interview?"

I looked at Nikki with a questioning look. "What's that?"

Nikki replied, "She means beer, Sistah," and at that moment I knew that this was going to be a costly trip. Nothing comes free. I agreed and sent Nikki to the store with Martie. Things were getting more upbeat.

While they were out, Lucius Jr. and I chatted for a while, waiting for the beer to arrive. I thought how alcohol could be as destructive as crack cocaine in the physical body. These relatives appeared thin, tired, and wore out. Lucius Jr. just looked at me with a blank stare. The moment was interrupted when they came back from the store.

I began explaining the details about the cubbyhole, the blue truck, and the bathroom. He said, "Where did this happen?"

The Dingahs and I all said at the same time, "Maffitt Street!"

He just shook his head. He began to talk about how we was raised up not to go nowhere with nobody. The kids today do what they want to do, no matter what they are told.

I said that was true, but it's one thing for a girl to give herself, and another for a man to force her.

He said, "I never had no experience with none of that. I never heard nothing about it either. When I was young cousin Miles came over, loaded all the dishes from the cabinets onto a heavy tray, and told me to carry it.

'What you want me to do with it?' I asked.

"Miles said, 'Put it down. Pick it up. Put it down.' Then he went down the line having all of us young men lift the tray.

"Then Miles said, 'Go get in the car. You're ready for a job.'

"After that, he got jobs for me and Baker Boy and Harry's sons and other boys in the family. We were working in hotels and restaurants.

"Dale had a problem getting that up-close-personal money. I would empty the ashtrays, wipe the tables, and ask people if they needed anything…I went the extra mile to get the tips. But Dale was the militant, talkin' about 'the white man this,' and 'the white man that.' He didn't understand.

"I used to go get Ted Jr. all the time to keep him working. He used to pull sting operations with my brother Dale and Uncle Harry's boys."

Lucius Jr. paused for a minute then he said, "I remember this one time that Ted Jr., Dale, and Denny, Baker Boy's son, stole Grandma Mattie's money, a large amount. When my daddy caught up with them, he was going to whup them. I told them that Ted Jr. didn't have nothing to do with it. He was with me. My daddy asked me if I wanted my butt whupped too. I turned to Ted Jr. and said, 'I'm sorry, cuz. I tried to help you out.'

I listened with interest to his stories, but now I wanted to shift the conversation to the real subject at hand. I went on to tell him about Auntie Cedra's abuse by Kent and Ted Jr. . His response was, "If she had spoke up about it, perhaps it wouldn't have come down to you."

I said, "She told Grannie Gran about my abuse, but nothing happened. So she felt she didn't stand a chance in hell. You are right about more of us speaking up for ourselves, but really the adults should have been standing up for us."

I made sure Lucius Jr. understood that our uncles and brothers were taking us to the same location to molest us, and asked how could nobody see or know or do anything? He seemed to search himself for an answer.

He said, "At that time, life was hard. My mama Bertha was dead. My father wasn't really there for us. We spent a lot of time at Grandma Mattie's house. Perhaps part of the problem was there were no males in charge. As a child, you do what you're told. If you grow up with people doing sexual stuff to you, you don't know that it's wrong. These are the people you look up to. So this seems normal, until you grow up and find out it's not right."

I asked him did he know what happened to my mama Brenda when she was little. He said, "Nah, she never discussed nothing with me. She was my older cousin, my babysitter."

Aritha said, "She was raped by Hardy, Liza's husband."

Lucius Junior's response was, "That's why he went sick in the bar and fell off the stool dead."

I didn't expect him to say that. It confirmed other testimonies. Then the Dingahs said, "Guess who Hardy's child is?"

Lucius Jr. looked at Aritha and said, "Who? You?"

The Dingahs laughed and said, "No, Wanda is."

He answered, "Huh?"

I turned to Martie and asked her if she wanted to say anything. In my mind I thought, after all, she already charged me. At first she seemed like she had something to say, but she changed her mind. I gave her my phone number just in case. But then she said, "In those days people just didn't talk about this stuff. They just covered it up."

"Of course," I replied. "You steal the voice when you silence it. And guess what? The next generation's voice is silent too. And then the grandchildren. But the Lord said to expose the truth."

Martie nodded and said, "You're right. That way everybody knows who's not to be trusted."

I said, "I want you to understand that we're not here to beat somebody down with sticks and stones. We really want to tell them that Jesus loves them, and so do we, and if they ask for forgiveness, He will forgive. No forgiveness is needed from us. We just want to tell our stories, hoping that it will help someone else."

I turned to the Dingahs and said, "Ain't that right?"

"Yeah," they said.

Lucius Jr. said, "It's a good thing that everybody didn't know about that back then. I used to want Ted Jr. to come back home, but now I don't. Not just because of what you've told me, but what he did to me. He stayed in my house one time and stole all the food out of the fridge and my pistol. That really brought 'serendipity' between us!"

He sat back and took a slow drag on his cigarette, looking into space. "Also he wouldn't come back and take care of his own mama when she needed him. I called my auntie Nikki every day. It was the only number I knew because it never changed."

Most people in the room broke out with, "Franklin 13354!" and then we cracked up. At first Aritha doubted it, but I told her I would bet her birth certificate on it. Then we laughed because her birth certificate had no name on it.

The conversation turned into a discussion about boys and girls sleeping in the same beds. Martie said, "Sometimes there just aren't enough beds."

I said, "Yeah, but you need two beds, boys in one, girls in the other."

Nikki seemed disturbed by this. I know she has a lot of children, and she does the best she can. She said, "It wasn't our generation being the problem."

But I said, "The ones slightly older than us were the problem. Grannie Gran's kids were molesting each other." Then she understood.

A hush had fallen over the room. I can only guess that we were all picturing horrible scenes.

Lucius Jr. said, "Yo mama was the number one culprit. She taught others how to hustle, steal, lie, and get over."

Mama kind of smiled, holding her head to the side as if she knew all that she had ever been and done was quickly being unraveled right there in front of her children. But Then Lucius Jr. went on to talk about Ford, Grannie Gran's youngest son, and how he was gifted but had numerous women and children and didn't stay home to take care of them. It somehow bothered Lucius Jr. that Ford was still hanging in the streets at all hours of the morning.

"Ain't nobody out there then unless they hustling—all the liquor stores are closed. Ford's too old for that. My god, he got grandchildren. He can be out making money, but he's also making a lot of babies. I don't know what is wrong with Nikki's kids. Hell, even Uncle Mick and Kent strung out on heroin. Uncle Mick used to go downtown to the lawyer's office, get thousands of dollars, and come back with drugs. Hey, I've done coke. But he used to tell me don't ever put this needle in your arm."

Lucius Jr. made a joke. "Well, I learned something today. Glad you came by."

We kissed, hugged, and took a few pictures. The Dingahs, Mama, and I left. We got a call from Dale who was now home. We discussed the information we had gotten as we drove to Dale's.

So far, I was counting my journey as a success. Instead of interviewing individuals, I was doing families, but thank God, I was not alone. The Dingahs were with me. This last interview was costly, both in money and in energy.

As we headed toward Dale's I searched my thoughts. I wondered if I could keep telling the same story over and over again. I wondered if I was leaving anything out, or asking the wrong questions. I knew that I had to be diligent and keep the faith, because people were depending on me now to tell their stories.

Dale's girlfriend answered the door with a warm welcome. Dale came into the living room, and we all hugged. It was something familiar about being in his presence. The minute I heard his voice, parts of my childhood that I had forgotten called out to me, and I felt at home. I shared with them about the book I was writing about the family.

Dale leaned forward, pushing his thick glasses up on his nose. "You know, the problem with this family here is they're all a bunch of crooks."

That was not what I had expected to hear. He went on to say, "The biggest crook is sitting right over there next to you." And he pointed at my mama.

He said, "She was the main culprit in teaching folks, including me, how to rob and steal. Man, she could hustle."

We all looked at her. She was hanging her head waiting to hear whether we would be outraged or on her bandwagon. It seemed everywhere we went she was being implicated in the family's patterns of dysfunction. Lucius Jr. had just told us the same thing. Who was this woman, I thought, whose voice was supposedly so silenced.

Dale said, "And her mother, my own mother's sister, wasn't no better. She kept food locked up in the cabinets. She showed favoritism to both Ford and Crystal, and made sure they had what they wanted. She would do things for them she wouldn't do for the other kids, and some of them were her very own. I remember one time when Ford went upstairs and asked her for a baloney sandwich. He came downstairs eating a sandwich. My brother Sam went upstairs and asked for a sandwich. She said it wasn't no more baloney. Now mind you my mama is dead, and she our auntie, supposed to take care of us! I was high off of PCP. I went and got a meat cleaver, came upstairs, and kicked her door in.

"I said, 'Ain't no more baloney, huh? I want all the money in here, and I ain't playin.'

"She said, 'I ain't got no money. Let me go next door and get some from the neighbors.'

"I busted the TV with the meat cleaver. 'What you think this is, the movies?' I yelled at her.

"Ford, her own son, came in the room and started searching and pulling money from little hidden places. Then my brother Cain came to the door.

"I said, 'Cain, you don't want to come in here. Anybody come in here ain't leaving.'

"Nobody could call out or in—I cut the phone wire before I kicked the door in. That's how high I was. Sam ran somewhere and called my daddy, Lucius Sr., and he showed up. I said, 'Daddy, don't come in here, 'cause you ain't leavin' either.'

"Daddy asked, 'What you want, son?'

'I want money. I got to get back to California.'

"Daddy turned to Grannie Gran and said, 'How much do we have?' meaning of her little change they had gathered.

"'About seventy-five dollars,' she said.

"'Come on son, let's go,' Daddy said. I followed him out to the car, sitting behind him with the meat cleaver, like I was still in control. We got to my daddy's house, and the next day he called Nikki (Grannie) and told her to get everybody out of the house, 'because Dale would be coming back to get his stuff.'"

We were laughing while he was telling this story, but at the end, I asked him, "Dale, would you have really hit my grannie with that meat cleaver?"

"I will never know. If Sam hadn't called my daddy, the drugs might've took over. In those days, we was desperate. Our mama was dead, and our daddy didn't really take care of us, so we was on our own. We didn't care if our blood hit the ground. It was all about getting some money."

I took a deep breath and plunged in. "Did you hear the rumors about my grannie and your daddy?"

"Oh yeah," he said. "I even heard Crystal could be his daughter."

"I heard that, too. She told me that when she was on crack, he took advantage of her. He knew she would do anything for money, even turn tricks with him. And she did," I said.

Everybody was quiet. Dale said he believed it, but that was his daddy, and he loved him.

He said, "When I grew up, there wasn't a picture of my mother nowhere. I didn't know what she looked like. One day when I lived in California, my brother Sam had came for a visit. He pulled a picture out his pocket, and it looked like an old 1920s picture."

"'Who's that?' I asked.

"Sam said, 'It's your mama.'"

Dale smiled at the memory.

He went on to talk about his mother's death. He was convinced that the abortion killed her.

I went on to ask, "What is the hostility between your daddy and Marie?"

He said, "Marie took my mother for the abortion."

I said, "Marie told me she was tricked into it, that she drove but thought the other girl was the one getting the abortion."

He said, "Oh no, Marie's not getting off the hook. Her other brother KW and his wife Ginnie knew all about it, too. She was a street woman. She knew everything about the streets. Her and my auntie Dam and my mama were all buddies, goin' to clubs together. Marie was the college girl. You know they knew where all the little places was to get abortions. First, my mama asked Ginnie to take her, but she said no. She didn't want to get involved. She told Bertha to go ahead and have the baby, and leave Lucius Sr. alone. But no, she was determined to get rid of it. So Marie took her to the back alley place. That's the story I heard. Also Kent told me she had a gum disease in her mouth that might have killed her as well."

"Yeah, tell me more about Kent," I said eagerly.

"Kent was quiet, the sneaky type. You know he shot that stuff all the time after he came back from Vietnam. All I can remember was after Mama died Grandma Mattie kept all the kids. My other Grandma, Annie Mae Lawson, never kept us, and maybe that's why they hated each other. Both sides of the family never clicked. My auntie Dam said my daddy used to give her money to buy us clothes. She dressed us nice and sent us to your Grannie Gran's house on Maffitt St. She sent us back wearing dirty clothes that belonged to her kids, so my auntie started to send us down there raggedy, thinking maybe she'd send us back dressed right." He laughed.

I asked him did he think it was possible that Grannie and his daddy were messing around before his mama died. First, he said that maybe that's what it was all about, or it could have been this lady Margaret.

Dale looked thoughtful and said, "I remember Margaret being around a lot right after my mama died."

I had been sitting in his house for over an hour, and I noticed something different about him. He used to drink a lot when I was young, and he had talked about alcohol, but he hadn't had a single drink.

I said, "Dale, you don't drink no more?"

Aritha said, "Dale was always so real even before he stopped drinking. He used to give and give and give...but now, when you ask him for something, he's like, 'I ain't got it...'"

He said, "I can't understand people who drink. They supposed to be giving to people, but these people be stingy."

"Are you getting tired of all these questions I'm asking?" I asked.

"No," he said.

"I'm testing my own memory," I said, "to confirm the truth about stories I heard in my childhood. This family is very secretive, yet the truth keeps breaking through. By the way, did you know Horse?"

"Yeah, that's Ted Jr.'s daddy's brother."

"I heard he had two sons that are in the penitentiary."

Dale said, "Yes, they killed a family viciously. I think they were high. They came over Grannie Gran's house dressed as girls shortly after they committed their crime. They were trying to hide. Eventually, they turned themselves in. One of them wrote and published an article in prison."

"Do you know who my father is?" I asked.

"Hardy?" he asked.

I said, "Yes." This turned into an emotional outburst from my mother.

"Yeah!" she said angrily. "Liza just didn't believe me neither!" She then told her story of being raped at fifteen by Hardy. My sisters and I were shocked at her outburst. We had discussed before we left home to stay on track with our interviews and not get emotional or sidetracked.

I was glad for what Dale said to mama, "It doesn't matter whether Liza believed you or not because Liza wasn't the one who raped you."

I grew tired suddenly of hearing myself asking questions and hearing almost the same answers everywhere I went. After my mother's outburst, I thought it best to stop now and continue tomorrow. I asked Dale if he would be available, and he said yes. We did our kissing and hugging and left.

In the car, I had to confess to the Dingahs how overwhelmed I was, with all we were learning about the women in the family and the male role models. We were all feeling pretty down. The best we can figure is that most of Grandma Mattie's children died early. It wasn't their fault they died young, but it created a hardship for Mattie to try to raise so many grandchildren. It seemed there was no positive role model for the boys. However, Mattie was one of the first black women to own property and businesses in her neighborhood. In a sense, her children robbed themselves of their inheritance by literally stealing from her and draining her resources and her energy. Everybody was out for himself.

The car was silent on the ride home. I dropped off Aritha then drove to Nikki's house. Jody was there, so I let her spend the night. She and Nikki's daughter Bonnie got along really well. Finally, Lavita, Mama, and I got to the house. Despite our exhaustion, Lavita and Mama got into an argument as usual. I told them to shut up. Arguments were always breaking out in our family, and seemed to go nowhere. I was too tired to be a social worker or a referee at that moment.

The next day we all woke up happy and friendly. The phone rang. It was Gene, Aritha's husband, who wanted to know if I could pick his mother up and bring her to his house when I came. This was the day of the month when people got their checks, and the mailman hadn't come by Mama's house yet. I went and got Miss Grace and brought her back to Mama's house. She and Mama were very close, like two peas in a pod. They had the same kind of spirit and liked to do the same things.

Vita and I sat outside on one bench and mama and Miss Grace sat on another. We were having separate conversations. Vita and I were talking about the things we were learning about Mama and how it disturbed us. Before we knew it, Mama was telling one of her stories. We listened as she talked about robbing a store by taking up the floorboards above it and dropping down into the store. She coerced some of the young boys in the family to help her. I remembered this store from when I was a little girl. The man was good to our family. He used to give Grannie Gran cash for the store coupons, and give us things on credit. As Mama bragged, I told her that if this were 2006 she would be busted. Nobody is that stupid. She'd have been the first person they investigated, with those loose floorboards.

I asked her, "Why are you glorifying something you should be ashamed of? A person who is saved asks the Lord to forgive them when they testify about their past. But you're acting proud of what you did."

Lavita and I got up, so overwhelmed at that moment that we went inside. We looked at each other with embarrassment and disgust. Then some white haired old lady told us on the elevator that things were going to be all right and to stay encouraged. I knew that was a sign from God.

We all headed to Dale's house. Dale was eager to see us this day. I guess he had some time to think about yesterday's conversation. He jumped right in.

"When we was growing up without a mama, I don't think we got the love and stuff that other people got. You know a mother give you a little bit of this here, and daddy give you a little bit of that there. I just lost that part. Me and Harry's sons used to go around and fight folks because they'd talk about our mama. Ironically my mama was dead, and so was theirs."

I was also ready to jump right in.

"Did you know," I asked, "that your sister Cassie is Grannie Gran's ally? She keeps her deep dark secrets locked up like a teddy bear." I watched for his reaction.

Dale ignored me and turned to mama. "Brenda, you was the big sister. Crystal was the smallest, and Cedra was the middle. She had it rough."

Mama broke out in a jealous rage, "She ain't had nothing rough."

That brought out a crude laughter among us, but we all agreed with Dale that she did have it rough.

Mama said, "She ain't never appreciated nothing you do for her."

I said, "Mama, you're looking at it from just your point of view."

Dale said, "She got involved with men and had a child when she was real young. Cedra was some cocky gal. She would knock a brother out. She really wasn't no pretty gal, you know. Living on Maffitt Street, she was embarrassed to bring people there. Just let me say this here—Nikki, know I love her. She done got old, and if she need anything, she can call me. What really messed up her kids was her concentration on Ford and Crystal. They could do no wrong."

She was busy tending her forty-five year secret love affair, instead of all of her children, I thought, and they ran rampant, robbing and molesting.

Dale continued, "Lil Ford used to want to run with me. I told him he was too young. But he ended up in the game anyway—it's in his blood. Like I said—crooks!"

Dale looked over at Aritha. "You wanna play?"

She reached into her purse and brought out a deck of cards. I thought she had quit gambling, but she surely hadn't. She shuffled the cards, and then shuffled them again.

Dale said, "Deal the cards." She continued shuffling and then she told him, "Money on the wood, make the bet good." Dale laughed.

"You taught me that," she said. "We were playing cards, and I won. You didn't pay me. Instead, you taught me a lesson, so now—put your money on the wood, so the bet will be good." And so he did.

I was almost afraid this was going to take all afternoon. Once these folks started gambling, it was over. I sat and watched for a while, and then decided that it was as good a time as any to ask Dale about the molestations on Maffitt Street.

Once again, I told him my story about Kent molesting me and Auntie Cedra. I also told him about Ted Jr. and Auntie Cedra and my sisters as well. He listened as they played cards, then he stopped and cleared his throat.

"I don't know *nothing* about that. All the people I hung out with, we was about getting some money. We were known as the Dillinger gang. People hired us to rob, assault, burn down houses—all the dirty work. That's what we were about. Now Ted Jr. tried to hang with us, but he wouldn't hurt nobody."

I asked him if they were the ones wearing the blue overalls with the red scarves hanging out the pockets. He said yes. I remembered that from my childhood. Then he went on to say that Grannie's brother KW knew about insurance scams, and Baker Boy, her other brother, knew a lot about the law. The two of them together pulled many capers for money, and also taught us how.

Aritha said, "Gotcha," and picked up the money on the table. For once, the game ended early. My memories of him when I was little were that he always had a beer or a joint with him. Now he wasn't drinking or smoking weed.

"I'm addicted to Pepsi, coffee, and Jesus," he bragged. Then he commented, "I eat meat. What do you drink? Milk?" As a Christian, I knew what he meant. He was calling me out to see if I really was in Christ. I told him that I don't drink much milk any more, and that I've been eating meat for the past fourteen years.

He replied, "Everybody can't eat meat."

I said, "The Lord has had me in the palm of His hand for fourteen years. I am filled with the Word of God. I may not be able to flip to every scripture given, but the Word lives inside of me and His Spirit gives me understanding. It keeps me from being cocky and keeps me stayin' in my place. I am a seasoned Christian, but sometimes I have to go back to remember where God brought me from. I've learned what to chew, what to spit out, and what to digest." Dale laughed.

Dale also made an accusation against Marie, saying she was Kent's payee and he got a large settlement plus monthly stipends from his military service. She would dribble out small amounts to him. So what if he was on drugs? It was his money. He was always crying broke, but had money. Dale said he thought that Kent followed Marie to California because she had the purse strings.

"Most everybody was working to support Marie's college

education," said Dale. "I believe that Marie used other people's money in the family to prosper. She did try to help the family, and of course, they all took advantage of her, including myself. That's 'cause we all crooks!"

Everyone had a good laugh. We all recognized the truth about ourselves.

Dale said, "Marie used to put me out the house but what she forgot was that I broke in houses for a living. When she'd leave, I'd go back in. When it was time for her to come home, I'd go back out.

"One of these times Marie put me out I decided to go up to Mount Tam. I made sure I took my malt liquor with the bull on it. Now I knew that every time I got drunk the bull chased me. So this time I took my red drawers with me. I got undressed, hung my drawers on a tree, so this time when the bull came after me, he'd chase the red drawers. So I was butt naked, lying down on the ground, drunk. I was dreamin'. I saw myself in a casket. Then all of a sudden, I woke up, and there was the devil. He was raisin' the dead.

"I got so scared I ran down the hill about eighty miles an hour. All of a sudden, I heard the police sirens comin' down the hill after me. The cop pulled beside me and told me I was running eighty miles per hour, and I was naked. What was wrong? I said that instead of a bull chasing me I saw the devil raise the dead. He locked me up. Of course, I called Marie. She got me out."

This story had us howling. I forgot how funny Dale could be. His girlfriend asked us if we'd like another soda, and we took bathroom breaks. Dale said, "I got two more things I want to tell you. In reality, it was my brother Sam I saw dead in the casket, and that my drinking caused me a lot of trips to the jail house. But the last time I went, I heard the Lord's voice. He said to me, 'Born a sinner.' Then he gave me a poem that changed my life. Dale gave me his permission to use it. It's funny though. I didn't know anything about Martin Luther King and the Freedom Riders, but God used that to change me."

Dale's Poem

I was born into sin from the very start,
The older I got the more it filled my heart.
I had to do something and I had to do it fast
My time was running out if my life was to last.
I had but one chance but was it for me?
It was Christ Jesus who set me free.
I asked myself, how could I be so bold?
For I was a thief who lied and stole.
But I remembered that because of God's good will,
The Lord Jesus Christ had paid the bill.
I confessed to the Lord Jesus and he came into my heart
He cleansed it and gave me a new start.
Delanor Powell (AKA) Dale

FAMILY GATHERINGS

The next day was our mini family reunion. We had invited some of the relatives we had visited and interviewed. We even saw Kelly at a gas station and invited her. She is Dale's baby sister, and she once lived in California with me and Marie, before the other girls came. But it didn't work out for her and she went back to St. Louis.

We were all dressed up in the Dingah Sistah shirts I had made before leaving home. However, my nieces decided to personalize them and have the Dingahs sign the backs of everybody's shirts with the number 1, 2, 3, and 4 according to who was born first. We had a feast at Nikki's house.

Parties don't always have the crowd you expect. That's what makes parties…parties. The biggest surprise was when Rob Lee Sr. showed up with his other family. Now this is Mama's ex-husband that who was the father of most of her kids. This is where the party got interesting. It was Rob Lee Sr. birthday. I hadn't hung out with him in many years. He had aged and was not the number one stunner he used to be. That man used to have a lot of women, but now he didn't even have teeth in his mouth.

My attention then turned to the two mamas. Rob Lee Sr.'s present wife, Tasha, was quiet, and seemed to avoid being in the room where Mama was. My sisters told me that they didn't know what was wrong with Mama, that normally she and Tasha were on friendly terms. *Perhaps it was because I was there, stirring up old stuff. Perhaps it was because of the smoke and her asthma. Oh well.*

All of a sudden, an argument broke out between Mama and Rob Lee Sr. He seemed to be defending himself against Mama's anger. She lashed out at him, something about him not being no good and a crook, and he agreed that he was a crook but that she had tried to out crook him and got crooked. After hearing this exchange, I decided that interviewing him might be quite interesting. So I invited myself to his house on Monday evening, and he agreed. Even though I wanted Mama to reconnect with her feelings, I knew better than to bring her along on this interview.

I later asked Mama what was their argument about. She said he had made a comment that she didn't need to be in the room with all that smoke, and she felt he was trying to boss her around. She thought he should be bossing his own wife. I asked her did she still love him. She said yes. I asked her was it a romantic love. She said no, he was just the kids' dad. I asked her if she cheated on him. She said no, but I knew that given the birthdays of Nikki and LaVita are less than a year apart, something was fishy.

As the evening went on, Mama and Tasha continued to avoid each other, but the highlight for me was watching Rob Lee Sr. standing there, cutting cake, with the children and the grandchildren of his two families laughing and joking and playing together around him. That moment was beautiful and priceless.

That night Mom was very talkative about Rob Lee Sr. and his various affairs with women. She recalled how violent he had been with her, and how he had never been faithful to no woman, then or now. A sadness fell on her face when she talked about our baby brother Mick who died of crib death. Soon after that Rob Lee Sr. had picked up another girlfriend, Betty, who had a son by him named Patrick at the same time Mama had Nikki.

Mama said she was married to Rob Lee Sr. but can't remember or didn't know if they were ever divorced, because she never signed no papers. Since then he had been married several times, and so had she. She now realized that he never cared about women at all. In fact, over those years, she got a lot of phone calls from other women who were just as foolish as she was.

It was Monday morning, and I had scheduled an interview with Lucius Sr. My heart was pumping fast as I sat in Appleby's waiting for him. He was over an hour late, but LaVita and I had arrived late as well, and we were beginning to think we'd missed him. I called him, and the first time he answered. He said he was "way across town near Lucius Jr.'s house," and he would be coming in about forty-five minutes.

LaVita said, "Wait a minute! He's lying. Lucius Jr.'s house ain't way across town. He lives on Maffitt Street two blocks from 4014." After forty-five minutes, we knew we was duped! So we ordered breakfast. I was full of disappointment. He could have made up an excuse, or just said he didn't want to be interviewed. He never showed up. I imagined him sitting with his cigar clenched in his teeth, nodding and saying to Grannie, "Yeah, I got 'em, baby."

After Appleby's we picked up the rest of the Dingahs and were off to Rob Lee Sr.'s house. Keggie was with us. Aritha was upset. She told me that Mama and her mother-in-law would do the same thing every time they would come to her house. They would arrive with a small bag, and leave with a big fat carry-on. They would take her towels, her food, and whatever they wanted. Most of the time, she would go to their houses and take it back. I knew exactly what she meant. It was my mother too.

Rob Lee Sr. was anxious to see us and welcomed us into his back yard. St. Louis summer nights are beyond beautiful, except for those mosquitoes. Keggie was already on a beer run, and I was excited to get started. I believe Rob Lee Sr. was relieved I didn't bring my mama. She didn't like being left behind, but I needed to do this without her comments. I clicked on the tape recorder. There are always several sides to a story, and I was there to get his.

"Rob Lee Sr., you had a lot of women. They sho' loved you," I began.

"I admit that," he said with a smile.

"Exactly how many kids did you have?"

He started counting. "T'ree, six, nine …" We all started to laugh.

"And how many different women did you have these children with?"

"T'ree."

"Did you have a son named Patrick?"

"Yeah."

"Mama said he was born at the same time in the same room as Nikki," I said boldly.

He raised his voice, "Dat's a lie!" His missing teeth in the front of his mouth allowed the wind to travel through as he spoke.

"Weren't her and Mama friends?" I asked.

"Dat's anudder lie!"

Nikki spoke up, "My birthday's on the seventeenth, and Patrick's is on the twenty-first."

"Dey din't come friends til' af'er you was born," he said to Nikki.

I asked him, "Why such a tight knit circle, Rob Lee Sr.?"

"Ah don' know. God know I cain't take back what I did."

"Do you have any regrets?" I asked.

"No, no, no," he said, face down, shaking his head left to right with his eyes closed, like he was trying to convince himself.

"What did you know about Grandma Mattie?"

"Ms. Ford? Nothin' really. She was always good to me, treated me all right. We lived in her basement when we first got married over on Saint Ferd'nand."

Nikki screamed out, "I bet you know plenty about Grannie Gran, don't you?"

Rob Lee Sr. looked at her and smirked, "Oh, yeah."

I added, "You said something at the barbeque about Mama and Grandma being crooks. What'd you mean?"

"I was just messin' wit' her," he said.

I thought to myself, *Out of the mouth, the abundance of the heart's condition speaks.* I pressed on. "So what about Grannie Gran?"

"Dat's the thing. When we first got married, Ms. Nikki was getting a check for Brenda. She told me she was gonna report dat Brenda was married to stop da check, because it was comin to her in care of Brenda. But she din't do it. She kept getting it ev'ry month for Brenda."

I realized that probably that was the reason SSI was taking big chunks out of Mama's money every month.

Rob Lee Sr. said, "I was mad with her for that. We was havin' hard times, and she wouldn't give her none of dat money." His face grew mean with his rage. "Ah mean *hard times.*"

Nikki shouted out, "Yeah, Grannie Gran used to take Bag's check all the time, too. Baggs used to say, 'I gotta buy my grandma medicine,' and he would walk long distances and pay for it himself. One day he got caught stealing batteries. Every time he got caught stealing it was for batteries. He always kept a radio with him, and Cain did too."

Aritha shouted in the background, "Crooks!"

I thought about Cain again. I used to get the same eerie feeling I got around Kent and Baker Boy. But Cain was disabled, and he couldn't catch me, so I wasn't worried about him.

Now I was ready for deep water. I told Rob Lee Sr. I remembered him beating my mama while I watched. I asked him why he beat her.

"Yo mama used to start da fights. She just loved to fight," he said.

"I used to have a fear of dark men, and I think it was because of those fights," I said. "Just watching you towering over Mama, your dark skin seemed evil to me, and being a child, it struck fear in my heart."

"Now I know why I love to fight," said Nikki. Just then Keggie arrived with the beer. Everybody snatched one and took a break. I went to the bathroom. I could hear them through the window, laughing and shouting and talking over each other, ghetto and fabulous. I couldn't help wondering, who am I fooling? These are my folks, and I'm just like them. I remembered myself as a child, watching a lot of TV, and I had a favorite show called the "Flying Nun." When I would fall asleep, I would dream about being the flying nun. Everybody in the town could look up and see me flying around. There was nobody else who could do that except me and the flying nun. It was my way of escaping reality, yet today I feel like I'm flying again, soaring above my circumstances, saving the day.

I went outside and sat down. I looked at Rob Lee Sr. and said, "So, Dad, were you aware of the unhealthy conditions that your children were living in? There were many times when I visited that there was no light or electricity, running water, hardly any food...?"

"All the bills were in all of our names because they was never paid!" said Nikki sarcastically laughing and falling out of her chair.

I was trying to stay focused, so I ignored the jokes.

Rob Lee Sr. betrayed a little shame as he looked at his feet and said, "I was givin' yo mama child support faithfully. I got no receipts from her, but her and Bean would go right up on Sarah Street and blow da money. Da kids would be at home, hungry. Sometimes dey even called me."

"Yup! Yup!" Aritha said. "And sometimes we would tell Mama we was gon' call our daddy, and she would scream at us, 'Call him! Go 'head and call him!'"

Rob Lee Sr. said, "Many time I'd go over dere, and the kids be by demselves. Dey'd be hungry. I'd take dem wit me. Den I got a problem wit dey mama and Bean."

I decided to move on to another question. "Did you know that every husband or boyfriend that Mama had was violent and beat up the children?"

He replied, "I never knew right off. It was dis time dat Baggs called me and told me dat Bean was trying to make dem eat dog mess. I was so mad I went lookin' for him. Me and my friend dem set outside da house all night, but he din't come home dat night. I even went back da next night. When he got out da car, I shot at him. I don't know how I missed him, two times. I was goin' kill him dat day." Rob Lee Sr. got up and started to pace around the yard, then went and got a beer. Meanwhile everybody was drinking beer and getting loud. Nikki started cussing. Daddy picked up the water hose and sprayed her right in the face. To tell the truth, I was shocked to see it, but nobody else seemed surprised. In fact, he sprayed her several times before that night was over.

Next I wanted to find out how much of a crook my mom really was. So I asked.

"Did Mama always steal things and con people?"

He said, "No, she learned dat later. But it used to make me so mad how people used to talk 'bout her. They called her 'triflin' and said she would go to bed wit anybody. I used to get into a lot of fights behind her. I had to stop goin' up to da club for a while. One time I had to take da kids away from her and Bean 'cause of da environment and da predicament dat dey were in."

"She said that you wouldn't let her see the kids at all."

"She lyin!" Rob Lee Sr. said angrily. "Dere was a problem ev'ry time she took the kids. She would fill deir heads wit nastiness bout me and Betty, things kids don't need to hear. Anything to make dem want to come back to her. Betty and I both worked, and when she would call home to check on da kids, the line would be busy so she had to do da emergency call to break in. Yo mama was on the line with the kids, saying 'NO, the hell with Betty!'"

"So dad, why did you and mama break up?"

"I was working at nights, yo Mama would be in da streets. I

had store credit at two stores so dey'd always have somethin' to eat. One of da stores I always owed just ten dollars. Da other store, your mama ran the credit up so high I couldn't pay the bill. Ah just got tired. She was lazy, and she wouldn't spend her money right. Also I think she was foolin' around. Baggs told me that Mama was in bed with Charles. Now I had a brother named Charles, and knew another guy, but I didn't know which one it was. One day I found a letter to Charles, and it said he didn't have to worry because she was goin' to put me in jail for child support. Dat letter hurt me. I kept that letter for many years."

Nikki broke in again—"You got it before she mailed it, huh Daddy?"

Everybody started laughing. It was getting late, and the mosquitoes were biting the heck out of me. I decided to call it a night, but asked if we could come back tomorrow evening. Everyone agreed.

The next morning the Dingahs decided this was the day we were going to hunt down an army truck and a soldier, and take some pictures. St. Louis had just had the historic flood of '06, and the national guards were driving through the center of town so much that Chickie got excited. We dressed up in fatigues and went looking. Right near Aritha's house we saw a sign on a street that said "Do Not Enter." We went on in anyway and saw a whole fleet of army trucks. We started screaming and shouting, "Where the camera? Come on, let's do it!" The courage of lions!

As we jumped out the car we saw across the street a group of men in civilian clothes. That wasn't what we was looking for, but we sweetly asked one of the men to take our picture by the trucks. And we did the Fool, posing and being silly. Mama sat in the car shaking her head. We never got a picture with a soldier together but on the way home I got a picture with a real honest-to-God MP in the airport. I got extra Dingah points for that.

Rob Lee Sr. and I continued our conversation the next evening.

"What did you know about Grannie Gran and Lucius Sr.?" I asked.

He laughed. "Lonnie used to always say that him and her was screwin'. Lonnie would get so mad he used to stay 'cross town with his wife, but both women knew about each other. It wasn't a problem. He couldn't catch 'em, but what man come to some woman's house late at night talkin' bout getting his hair done?"

I almost fell out with laughter, and so did the Dingahs. Rob Lee Sr. didn't get it.

"Lonnie stayed drunk most of the time."

Rob Lee Sr. continued, "That grandma of yours was something else. She used to cover for Liza. Every week a man would meet Liza there. Your grandma would have the room ready."

"Wait a minute," I said. "Are you sayin' Liza was "ho-ing?"

"Yeah."

I was silent. I remembered hearing she was cheating on her husband, but this was a whole nother different ball game.

"I used to see the trick coming down the steps," Rob Lee Sr. said.

"Did you ever hear that Crystal could be Lucius Sr's daughter?" I asked.

He said, "Naw. She looked just like Lonnie. But your grandma, she was a dirty broad, cold blooded and mean. When I found out that Brenda had a child, I wanted to take you out with us, but she wouldn't let me. Only one time did your grandma let you go."

"So she lied when she claimed that you were her boyfriend during her pregnancy with me?"

"Huh? She never even told me she had you for months."

I felt bad, but I went on to share a memory that I recalled from when I was about three. Rob Lee Sr. was walking proudly and I was riding on his shoulders, wearing a little red coat and matching bonnet, with two ties with furry black balls on the ends.

My hands were in a matching red muff with black fur on the ends. I remembered being happy and laughing.

Rob Lee Sr. looked pleased that I had a pleasant memory to share.

"I don't remember many things about my childhood. I've blocked out a lot of stuff, shielding myself from my memories of being molested. In fact, all of us were molested," I said.

"What?" Rob Lee Sr. asked. "By who?"

I told him our Dingah story. There was hurt in his eyes as he listened. I even told him about my conception by Hardy, and asked Rob Lee Sr. if he knew if Hardy had children.

"The man had two daughters, I thought," said Rob Lee Sr.

I reassured him that even though Rob Lee Sr.'s children had suffered, they were all right today. I then asked him how his grandma had treated his children. He said he knew she didn't like him. She had mistreated him when he was little, making him take off his pants and give them to his older brother. She fed the other children before him, and he could only eat if there was some food left over. And he would have to wash the dishes. She continued to abuse him as an adult.

"Why did she hate you?" I asked.

"I looked just like my grandfather. He had a gambling problem. So she took her frustrations out on your mama, my children, and me. When she got sick, guess who took care of her? Nobody but me. I used to tell my kids dat dey din't have to do things for dem because when dey get through wit what dey wanted dem to do, dey would send dem home. Dey just wanted to use dem."

I turned to my brother Keggie, who had mumbled something. He is hard to understand. "What?" I asked.

He didn't respond. I said, "If you only open your mouth and let the words come out, it would help you to forgive and be healed.

Running to the crack house won't help. You keep exposing

yourself to dangerous situations and act like you don't care about yourself."

Keggie nodded his head in agreement, but said nothing.

Aritha changed the subject. "I remember when Eve and Lena used to come to our house every Christmas when the city lights and trees went up. The two of them would find us no matter where we lived, even the time we lived in a three-story building, they climbed those steps and greeted us with open arms and a big hug, carrying baskets and bags full of gifts."

"Yeah, they looked out for us," said Nikki. "They're really our cousins but they act more like aunties."

Ritha said, "I never knew much about their kids, though."

I asked Rob Lee Sr., "Do men act stupid and make mistakes on purpose?"

He said, "Yeah, I've sho made plenty."

Time was getting late and there was still something important I needed to ask. "How did you feel when you found out Baggs was gay?"

He looked uncomfortable and said, "He was still my son."

I delved deeper. "How did you feel when you heard he had AIDS?"

"It hurt. I loved him. But I couldn't live his life. He had to live it for his self. I accepted it. I just hate that it went the way it did. Baggs was in the hospital. When I came in, he jumped up, hugged me, and said, 'Daddy, I'm sorry.' There was nothing I could do to help him."

"Was he openly gay?" I asked.

"Yes, after a while, but he had girlfriends, too."

Aritha said, "Yeah, I think he got it from his girlfriend, because his lover didn't even know he had AIDS…till I told him."

This launched a huge discussion around how AIDS got spread.

Keggie interjected, "It's just people doin' it with other people. You just need one woman."

"But," I said, "if she's got more partners than you, you got a big problem. In my opinion, it's all just sexual sin."

I was tired. I turned off the tape, and for the rest of the night we just enjoyed each other's company.

TRUTH BE SPOKEN

Two of the healthiest and wealthiest older women in the family besides Marie are Eve and Lena. These are the daughters of Liza. They were a few years older than Baker Boy so they escaped his abuse. However, they witnessed part of his corruption when he brought home young women. He was allowed to bring the women into the same bed and have sex with them in the presence of the children who were supposedly sleeping. Lena said she never understood why her mother would allow such a thing.

There was a sickness in the family—tuberculosis. One sister, Vera, died from it, and Baker Boy and Grannie Gran survived. They had also previously lost a brother named JC from rheumatic fever. The sisters believed that Liza and Grannie Gran allowed Baker Boy to get away with so much stuff because he was sick with TB. Grannie Gran claimed that she did not remember JC. I asked Marie if she remembered JC. She said yes. So I asked Marie why would Grannie say she didn't remember him.

Marie's reply was, "Maybe it's because she doesn't like to deal with anything emotional."

I said, "Marie, that's just not healthy behavior." And Marie agreed, saying that we both knew Grannie had experienced cancer, kidney disease, diabetes, high blood pressure, and blindness. I said, "She's still holding on, but it seems that maybe her secrets are killing her."

Recently, Grannie had laser eye surgery, and she could see again, but all of her secrets were still hidden inside. I still think about how she sits in her chair clutching her robe, just as she did when I was a little girl. To look at her you would think that she's weak, but that's her defense. I can see past her deceptions when she gets up and moves across the room with her walker. Instead of pushing it, she actually carries it and then thumps it down. The rhythm is "one, two, three, bump!" "One, two, three, bump!" To me it's symbolic—I'm a person who follows signs and wonders. I see that she's carrying a huge load that perhaps began small, but since nothing was done about it, it grew.

It takes a vast amount of strength to keep a lifetime of memories suppressed, especially when she is surrounded by the results. She has witnessed and been a part of so much painful drama, but she won't acknowledge it, or talk about it. She thinks keeping silent is keeping it hidden, but I am the result of her silence. And there's more than me.

I wonder what really happened to her that made her shut down and turn a blind eye. *Was she a victim?* I'm afraid to ask her, out of respect. I think it might give her a cardiac arrest. Grannie was known in the family as a care giver who took care of everyone's kids, but neglected her own by not keeping a closer watch on them—especially the boys.

Eve spoke once of praying to forgive Grannie because she was looking for her son, and he was at Grannie's house, and Grannie didn't tell her he was there. When she mentioned it to Grannie she had a nonchalant attitude, and that made Eve angry. She said she didn't understand how mothers turned their heads and ignored what was going on in their own homes.

I love and admire the way these two women and brother treat their mother. They take turns taking care of her since Alzheimer's has set in. They are finding out more things about her life and getting a better understanding of who she was and is. Both women told me that they had a brush with being almost raped, but somehow their attackers were scared off. They believed that they always had angels protecting them. They were encouraged to get an education and make good choices, and they did. In those days, people didn't lock their doors, but little did they know that there were dangers in their own homes.

How does a family pass on traditions, behaviors, and a way of life? Does the bad get passed on with the good? We try to hide the bad things about ourselves, thinking that no one can see them, but people—children especially—do see our faults, and especially the children see them. *There are no secrets in families, only silence.*

During the time that I interviewed them in St. Louis, the two sisters talked about their mother's going out at night and cheating on her husband, who was cheating on her. She of course talked about his cheating, and but thought no one knew about hers. The sisters both said at the same time, "Mother always said, 'Two wrongs don't make a right.'"

They also spoke about the gambling in the family. Of course, the children watched the elders in the family gamble, and wanted to do it themselves. They then passed it on to their children. *Who teaches their children to gamble consciously?* Gambling is a big issue in our family, causing a quiet destruction.

How did the gambling, the touching, and sexual abuse get started in the family? Who, when, where, and especially why? Marie said that she was never aware of the sexual abuse, but she felt that the women in the family, generation after generation, kept repeating the same destructive behaviors. Her explanation was a lack of education, poor choices, and laziness.

Our next interview was a luncheon at Eve's house in our honor. Eve, her husband, and Lena were there, and their brother Arnold, Rosa and her daughter, two grandchildren, Liza, my mama Brenda, and the Dingahs. These were some of the members of the family who had gone further in education. There are many sides to a family. We wanted to know what had worked for them in their lives, and how could we use that to better the futures of our grandchildren. For those who didn't know I explained a bit about why I was writing the book. I told them their input would be valuable. My goal and focus was how to guide the children into new life.

Rosa began speaking. "You must pull them toward the positive, to leave the past behind."

I asked, "Did crazy things happen to you?"

She said, "Yes, I had obstacles, but I was not molested."

"Your mother was Louise, right?"

"Yes. She died when I was a little girl. I knew if I wanted things I would have to get them myself, so I decided to get an education. If I stayed around negative people, I wouldn't go anywhere. I was raised by Grandma Mattie and my father's people."

Lena broke in. "I want you to talk to Marie, to find out about Grandma Mattie. She was a great role model. She was the first in our family to own her own home and have her own businesses. She was always working, and cleaning. I never saw her drink a single drink. Everybody else was drinking, but not her. In fact, all the women in our family were married to men who drank too much."

Marie told me many times that the women in this family had bad luck when it came to choosing men. Even Mattie's husband, Papa Ford, was a thief and had to be put out.

Rosa said, "Marie was an inspiration to many of us, because she stayed in school and always dressed nice. I told myself, 'I can do this.'"

Arnold broke in, "Well, role models is good, but there wasn't no role models for the men. Seems everybody was out of control, doin what they wanted to do. When you got misguided stuff, you got a mess. I'm not makin' no excuses, but it was *tough* on the men. Miles and me was about the same age, and we just stayed away. We knew what was goin on, but we wasn't no part of it. Kent ..." He stopped and shook his head. "Somethin' was bad in him. He just couldn't seem to...and Ted Sr. He wasn't no role model neither. He was a straight-up hustler. In fact, all the Simmons men was hustlers." Everybody had a good laugh. "A skillful salesman is a step away from a con man." I felt his eagerness to reveal the things he had kept silent about for so many years. He even admitted that he identified with the hustle himself, but he chose another road. He was a successful businessperson and father who put his children through school and was a decent role model for them.

Miles too had tried to keep the family going and be supportive, despite his own issues of explosive violence. He grew up with his sister Gloria in an orphanage, but he always encouraged especially the men to work and provide for themselves and their families. However, drinking, drugs, gambling, and hustling took a toll on the Simmons men.

Eve spoke up. "La Wanda. Our love for your family started with your mama Brenda. We used to keep her when she was little, combing her hair as if she was our baby doll. Her children were like our children too. But we had no idea that this abuse was going on. There was a lot of good things going on...on Maffitt Street. I remember being young and getting pregnant. I wanted to kill myself. I wanted to go to school. Nikki (Grannie Gran) kept me for three weeks. I ended up getting married and having four kids by the age of eighteen. It was hard raising those kids and working, but I did it because I had to do it."

"You became the first woman to be a stationary firefighter—setting the standard...how'd you do that?"

"Hard work and people encouraging me. My husband never asked me to work. I did it because I wanted to. My next goal was to be the first black female engineer in St. Louis. Honey, my plan was to retire at sixty-two. However, God had other plans for me. I got ready to take the test, and my son Rod was killed in an auto accident. I lost all my motivation. I just wanted to go to sleep again and not wake up."

The room was silent.

"How did you get out of that?" I asked.

"Having my own office space provided me the chance to grieve. I also met a woman whose faith encouraged me to talk to Jesus. I closed my door and prayed. Instead of studying for the test, I studied the Bible. I told the Lord I didn't blame Him, because He doesn't make mistakes."

"Even the most horrible things that happen in our lives lead us somewhere," I said.

Lunch was ready and we stood and came together to pray. Evelyn prayed for the forgiveness for our family, and for the Lord to be in our midst. She prayed that the book would be a success and unite us as a family, and for Grannie's trip to be safe.

After lunch, I felt there was still something missing, so I decided to dig a bit deeper. As we sat around the kitchen laughing and trading family stories, I noticed how much Arnold looked like Baker Boy, and I wondered why some of the men in the family were abusers, and some weren't. They were all raised in the same circumstances. What was different? All the married couples started out living in Grandma Mattie's basement.

"Has our family always been so separated?" I asked.

Lena said, "No, there was a time I used to bring Gloria's children to my house, but after an incident where one of the girls said she had to lock herself in the bathroom because one of the boys tried to touch her, I was through bringing them over. It was important to keep the girls safe."

That's how it's supposed to be, I thought.

Rosa said, "I remember something, but maybe this isn't the time to talk about it."

Everybody said, "Yes, this IS the time!"

"Well, I walked in on Baker Boy raping a girl in the bedroom, and Bertha was there. I heard her encouraging him to do it."

Arnold asked, "Are you sure it was rape?"

Rosa said sarcastically, "What would you call it if the girl was screaming and crying? After I saw that, it affected me profoundly, and I never wanted men to touch me. Also I was told repeatedly that if you let a guy touch you, you'll get pregnant. It changed my perception of what love and marriage would be. It stole my innocence."

Eve said, "Well, now that you mention it, I can remember that when I was a young girl, Baker Boy made a pass at me. I was so resistant; I wouldn't play that. He never came at me like that again. I never said anything to anybody."

We all just shook our heads. *There's the elephant in the room*, I thought to myself.

Eve went on to say, "We need strong male role models in the family. We need to teach it, and you should put that in your book. I'm glad you're doing this, because I shared something today that I've held secret my whole life. I was mad with myself and bitter with men."

"Me too!" said Rosa. After that, the conversation stayed on light topics and as it was getting late, we said our goodbyes and decided to work together toward a large family reunion.

That night I went out with the Dingahs, my mama, and Ford, and we had a blast, blowing off steam. As I crawled into bed, knowing I was leaving the next day, I thought how God had opened up doors and people had stepped through. I felt it was a cleansing for us all. After returning home, I got a phone call that Arnold had had a stroke while on his tractor and had passed away. I felt grateful that I'd met him again and that he gave me the gift of his story that he had carried so many years. I believe now his soul rests in peace.

WOUNDS DON'T HEAL SO EASY

For some reason Grannie Gran didn't want to go to St. Louis when I went, but less than a week after I came home she was scheduled to leave. The day after I got home my children threw a big barbeque. I was raw from my trip, and unfortunately, my children felt the brunt of that. I later caught myself and apologized.

Marie asked me to bring Grannie to her house, but I wasn't prepared to face her. I'm not good at faking. I was still processing my feelings about the things I had learned, and I was a little short with her. I know she normally plays the ends against the middle, but this time it was bad timing because I was very wounded. By the time we got to Marie's house, I had actually sounded off on her. When she saw Marie, she burst into tears and played the victim once again. If Jerri hadn't been with me I would have almost believed her myself. I ran downstairs and had my own outburst. I was outraged at her manipulations. Marie just hugged us both.

Grannie looked ten years younger as she prepared to go to St. Louis. I went by Auntie Cedra's house to drop off some nightgowns for her trip. She had so much spunk. I was compelled to ask her, "So, where you stayin', Grannie?"

Her first response was, "Here and there." Then she spoke in an authoritative voice, "I'm staying with Lucius Sr." Finally, after fifty years, she admitted to her relationship with him. How ironic, coming out of the closet so late in life. I wondered if she would get there and not come back.

She did come back, but got sick again. Grannie Gran went to the hospital with new symptoms: a blood infection and something wrong with her lungs. I watched her just lying in her bed, and I was wondering, "Lord, where is this going?" She kept saying she wanted all measures taken to keep her alive, yet at what point do we stop interfering and at least recognize that the end is near. There was no discussion of the truth. It was time for everyone to accept that death was near, and prepare.

Tessa was there at the hospital too. At first, she looked stunned when I walked in. She hesitated, but when I smiled at her, she threw her arms around me. She talked about her fashion show she was doing for plus-size women, survivors of breast cancer. They were her models, and she wanted to design lingerie that had implants in the bras. She was so enthusiastic about it, and so was I. We both had similar interests. Perhaps one day we could work together in business. I was pleased to hear that her brother Kelo released an album. His rapper name is Zeke. I laughed proudly. I was almost afraid to talk about my book, but somehow it came up, and Tessa wished me luck.

I went back and forth to the hospital, as much as I could. Grannie Gran was not getting any better. I was surprised to run into Sandra there, but she's not allowed at Auntie Cedra's house either, and that is—her mother's house. Marie told me that the doctors and the family were having a meeting to discuss the plan of action. They decided that in a crisis the plan was to do nothing because her liver was too far gone, her kidneys were not functional, and the cancer was untreatable. That is a hard choice, but it's not the hardest. The division of the family is the real crisis. God's plan for Grannie Gran is natural and is being revealed. It is exposing the weaknesses of our family. It is said that death will make you or break you. I hope if it breaks us, it will break us into pieces so God can reassemble us.

I did not go to the family meeting because I did not want to take the focus off of Grannie and onto me and my *book*. I do have a confession though—I don't think I was very supportive of Grannie in her last days. Sometimes I was almost afraid to go see her, because when I looked at her I had to look at me. So many emotions: love, anger, forgiveness, confusion. I'm learning about loving people unconditionally, even those who show you no truth, love, or respect. The past is still all mixed up with my present. I know that the Lord is with me in this struggle, because He has placed me here. My emotions do not need to be my shield. That is old behavior. I have to trust God like I've never trusted Him before. I hope to remember this when it's time.

I woke up Saturday morning with a great need to go see Grannie at the hospital. She was in dialysis, sleeping restlessly, and moaning. She was drifting in and out. I sat there about twenty minutes procrastinating. There were doctors and nurses around. Suddenly the pressure was upon me and I began to rub her hands. She smiled.

I leaned in and whispered to her, "Grannie, Grannie." She opened her eyes. "I have a message for you from my sisters."

"What's the message?" she said.

I said, "We forgive you, Grannie, and we want you to forgive us. I remember being sick as a child, and you were there. I'm here now for you."

She began to weep. "I saw Jesus," she said.

"Did you say you saw Jesus?" I asked. She pointed to her feeding tube, changing the subject.

After we went back to her room, I was doubtful if she really understood what I had said. When the nurse left, I got a wipe and gently wiped her face and mouth. She said to me, "You're wiping my mouth?" Then I knew she had understood.

"It's time for peace, Grannie. When Jesus comes, let Him in." I kissed her, sat with her a while longer, then I left. As I walked down that long hallway, I knew it would probably be the last time I saw her alive.

I received a phone call from Aritha in St. Louis the next night telling me Grannie had passed here in California. All hell began to break loose, but God still was in control. Grannie had left clear instructions about her wishes. She had even brought her burial clothes with her and made arrangements at the Mormon Church. There was a viewing at Auntie Cedra's house before Grannie's body was flown to St. Louis. It was a time of peaceful sharing, for the moment.

I called Tessa, since she and her sister Trina were in charge of the funeral arrangements. I respectfully asked if I could participate in the service, but Tessa said, "This is my grandma's funeral and I don't want no problems."

I replied that I am the first grandchild and I want to be a part of it. She objected, a few ugly words were exchanged, and the line went dead. I decided not to worry about it, make my travel arrangements, and get there. Surely, there would be a time for the family's words of expression.

CRUEL INTENTIONS

During my eight-hour layover in Dallas, I tried to write a poem, but my gift wouldn't flow. All the Lord gave me was First Corinthians 13, *Love*. I later realized that He was showing me something I needed to know, but I didn't see it then. In my most difficult moments of pain and loss, I still needed to love unconditionally, and not to lash out in rage.

I thought that the wake was supposed to be a quiet hour, but this one was lively. It's hard to see people and family you haven't seen in years and not want to greet and hug them. I can't do it like that. And apparently, I wasn't the only one. It was noisy but exciting, and I'm sure this was probably the best moment for Grannie. Tessa tried unsuccessfully to get people to quiet down, but it had a life of its own.

I went to the bathroom and I said one "Thank you Lord," and the spirit took over. I was in there praying and screaming out to God for twenty minutes. If you are sensitive to the spirit, you can't always control those moments. When I came out of the bathroom I was bombarded with stories of conflict in the family. I knew then why I was in the bathroom for twenty minutes. There were just a few unfriendly incidents, but other than that, the wake was rejuvenating—I felt reconnected with my distant family. Some of us exchanged contact information for future family reunions.

The next day I was not prepared for the hostility that Brenda,

Marie, and I received. I wore white, even down to my gloves, knowing that Grannie would like that. She always encouraged me to look my best. For me, black did not feel appropriate. White for me expressed the Light. Auntie Cedra and her family had arranged a Mormon service for Grannie, which they said is what she wanted. The first part of the service we were in a little room where only the immediate family could be there, but that didn't make sense because Grannie had at least forty-six great grandchildren. Marie was running late and almost missed it. They were starting without her.

The next part of the service we went into a second room, where it was cold and dead. Black folks don't go to Jesus like that! We gotta make some noise so he knows we're coming. The pastor spoke about he knew Grannie Gran for twenty years, but I didn't know who he was talking about! Then several teenagers spoke and sang. Now they might have known their grannie some, but they were just youngsters. Dale read a poem that he wrote, and it was beautiful. I leaned over and asked the pastor if I could say a few words, and he told me they had to stick to the program. I tried to explain that I was the first grandchild, with many behind me, but I am the first. He shook his head no. I got up and left. I could feel the rage and disappointment inside of me. My soul was rattled. Aritha came after me and asked me to stay, saying I had a right to speak, so I came back. I wasn't the only one unacknowledged on the program. My mama Brenda wasn't allowed to participate, nor Marie. Bebe was asked to say the prayer, and she took Marie up with her as a tag-along. Bebe told me that she felt uncomfortable doing the closing prayer instead of Marie, Grannie's sister. Her desire was to bring peace among us all, and her words reflected that.

After the closing prayer, I raised my finger. The tension in the room was thick. There was so much being left unsaid by family members who had walked with Grannie for over forty years. At that moment, I decided to back off. There were too many people ready to follow my lead. Out of the sides of my eyes, I saw feet patting and snarled looks. I sat down and wept loudly till it was over. The only noise in the place was the sound of my weeping.

Something came to my mind that one of the elders whispered in my ear at church. He said, "Just because the devil gives you a picture, you don't have to accept it." The word of God comes to me at the right time to strengthen, build, and encourage me to press on. I was so glad I didn't let my ugly impulses show. I can't remember how I got to the car, but Nikki took the keys and took over. I was broke down, but I was being carried by God, giving me some time to collect myself. I powdered my nose and straightened my hat, so to speak, and went in to the reception.

On reflection, I felt that I had made a fool out of myself, but God does use the foolish to confine all the wise ones. Some of my family greeted me warmly, and I relaxed. Lola had cooked a beautiful meal as usual, and people were sharing, joking, taking pictures. In this one hour, all differences seemed to melt away. I noticed that Mama hadn't arrived. I thought the limo would bring her, but everybody had to drive separate cars. When she came in, she was very upset because nobody had offered her a ride with the immediate family. They made her wait around and ride with Lucius Sr. who was delayed talking to the funeral director. I didn't know she didn't have a ride. This was another slight, which I found hard to ignore.

When it was time to eat, Eve gathered us in a circle for prayer. Thank God for prayer. Auntie Cedra was missing, arriving late. Upon her entrance, the tension in the air grew. After dinner, Cassie held up her hand to speak. She voiced her feelings of disappointment and frustration of the conflicts in the family.

"I wish Miles was still here. All this would have never happened. He helped this family stick together," Cassie said in a high-pitched angry voice.

People nodded in agreement. Then Bebe took over and guided us in "friendly fire" where everyone was allowed to speak freely. I was the first one she called on. I finally was able to speak about love and truth in our family, as well as the separations. I said that some of us aren't even welcome in each other's homes. I have no idea how people reacted, but I felt good about opening up and being obedient to the Lord.

The highlight of the reception was when Mama raised her hand. She said she wanted to ask her sister Auntie Cedra a question. Silence fell over the room. "Why did Lucius Sr. have to call me and tell me our mother was dead? That was your job. You claimed you didn't have my number, but you did, because you called me often."

Auntie Cedra said, "Your kids…is the reason we don't get along."

Mama replied, "What do my kids have to do with me and you? In the last ten years, you have only seen one of my kids. I love you, and we're supposed to stick together."

There was a long pause. Auntie Cedra looked around and saw that she was being watched. Finally, the words fell out of her mouth, "I love you, too. I hold these grudges and I have a forgiveness problem. I'm like Grandma Mattie like that. Once somebody has crossed me, I can't fool with them no more. God is working on me." And as quickly as she flew in, she flew out. I thought about it. In all the years I lived with Grandma Mattie, I saw other issues but never harboring resentment and unforgiveness.

I was leaning against a wall listening, and a woman came up to me. She said, "Sister, when you walked through the door at the homegoing the Lord told me to pray for you. He told me your spirit was heavy laden."

I caught a hold to her hand. I knew God had sent me help. She began to pray and prophesy in my life about things that she couldn't have known, even down to my book. She saw that I was doing what God told me to do. She told me to let go of my feelings, and that this was a training for me. All my dreams and desires for the community she spoke about. I began to cry out to the Lord for myself. I hate being scattered, not feeling the peace of God. It was a confirmation that I wasn't crazy. Yes, rejection is still my biggest downfall, but God is there to pick me up. The more I learn to surrender, the more I am changed. Practice is powerful.

At last, it was all over and I could just relax. I wanted to make the best out of the rest of my trip, and to salvage the positive family memories, like Marie's seventieth birthday celebration with family and friends. Bebe and her husband had secretly arranged a lavish surprise party for Marie. There were poems, songs, stories, gifts, flowers, a slide show, fabulous food, and much laughter and tears. When Marie entered the room and realized what was happening, she busted out into her hip swaying dance (which I had loved as a kid), singing "She's a Bad Maamaa Jaamma." Grannie arrived late and made her grand entrance, as if the party was for her. Her face was shining with a big grin, her hair was freshly done, and she had on a hot pink jacket with black slacks. She stood in the spotlight in the middle of the room while everyone cheered and applauded, and she just absorbed it. It was a glorious and magical evening for everyone. It was Marie's finest tribute, and Grannie's last great public appearance.

It was a couple of days before Mom and I had to fly back to California, so this gave me an opportunity to get my brother Keggie's testimony. He had hung out with us during this whole time, and that's the first time that had happened. I knew that he could be committed to something if he wasn't held back by his addictions. I took him and my sister Vita to Appleby's, which is a nice place to have privacy and talk. I only took Vita so she could record, but we really didn't need her because we propped the camcorder on the back of the seat. Actually, her technical skills were not what she claimed they were, and eventually I had to "fire her." She got lots of free meals and cigarettes out of the deal.

We ordered a big meal and I realized this was the first time that my brother and I ever really sat down and broke bread together. We only knew each other in passing. He's the only brother still living out of four. He was very calm and very willing to talk to me. I found out that he was forty years old, and he had a high school education. That surprised me. Sometimes you can make an assumption about someone from their appearance or how they carry themselves, but that might not be who they really are. I had been told that he was always a nervous boy, rocking a lot, mumbling and twitching, and never being still. Today he was quite the opposite—he was focused and seemed comfortable with me. I felt loved and protected just sitting next to my brother in fellowship. For me, I needed the innocence of a loving family relationship with a man.

"So, did you know anything about the abuse that was happening to your sisters?" I asked.

"No, the only abuse I witnessed was the whuppings that we all got from mama's boyfriends," he replied.

"Did you do things to deserve whuppings?" I asked.

"Yes, I was bad, but what we went through, like hanging us up on nails, was more than whuppings."

"Do you know why Bean hung you guys on nails?" I asked.

"No. He would just be mad."

"Well, what do you know about Ted Jr. and Kent?"

"They was always good to me. They played with me. But my real role model was Gene. He would talk to me and take me places like a dad.

"Tell me something about your real dad."

"Like what?" Keggie eyed me suspiciously.

"Was he there for you? Did he talk to you and take you places?"

"He was there, but he didn't take me no place. It was more like, he'd say he'd be comin but he never got there. He made a lot of excuses. But we did live with him off and on. He was into drinking, and women."

"Tell me about your crack addiction. What keeps you bound?"

He replied, "I been clean for a week now."

"Yes, that's good, but what's gonna keep you from going back out this time?" I asked harshly. "In fact, what made you leave the crack house where you were staying?"

He said, "Jay beat me up and put me out."

"Why?"

"'Cause I let somebody use his truck. They went and stole a generator with it, so he got mad."

"Why do you keep going back to crack? What are you running from?"

Keggie shifted around and seemed to be getting nervous, but I wasn't about to let up.

"Are you ready to face your fears? Keggie, what are you afraid of?"

"I don't know. So much has happened. I miss my brothers. First, my baby brother died of a hole in his heart when we were kids. Then my brother Stevie died on my birthday, and…he was shot in the stomach by his girlfriend's cousin who wanted money for drugs. Then my brother Baggs died of AIDS. I haven't been right since."

"Wow, that's a lot to carry," I said softly. "Is that why you got into drugs?"

"I guess I was looking for something to do. Gene and I were just experimenting. First, we started snorting, then when crack came along we went along with that, like everybody else. Gene stopped, but I couldn't. But Gene say he proud of my week clean. Now I want to stay clean for my grandkids. My daddy takes me over to see them sometimes."

"Is your daddy using too?"

"Yep. He be there at the crack house too."

"You get high with your daddy?"

"No, I won't do that. He be in one room, I be in another. Sometimes I can't get loaded because I gotta watch out for him. That house is crazy—guns, fights, all kinda of crazy stuff."

"Have you ever talked to your daddy about how you feel when you see him get loaded?"

"He ain't gonna listen to me. I'm doin the same things he is. But it hurts me to see him like that." Keggie was just shaking his head.

I reminded him that I had a crack addiction for over seventeen years, and that it is possible to quit. "I have fourteen years clean now. I asked God to heal me and He did. This is what this book is about—stepping into healing. Deliverance is right now. Just ask God ..." and we did the Sinner's Prayer right there in Appleby's.

Keggie has been back and forth since that interview. His last attempt he went to church four weeks in a row—that's a record. He fell off, went back over to the crack house, and just before he got there the police kicked the door in, but they never even saw him. The Lord is good! Even when we can't take care of ourselves, we need only ask and He will take care of us. Presently Keggie is at Aritha's house, he's clean, and he's going to church.

Every time I call St. Louis, I ask about him. It is such a joy when Aritha says, "Hold on, he's right here." I continue to try to encourage him to stick with it, that God will do it for him. These are some blessed times for us, even though many of us in the family are dealing with serious health challenges. We trust the Lord will bring us through. So many of us are getting saved, just like God said we would. I look forward to my next trip home to rejoice in what God has done. The sad news is Keggie is back in the streets using again. Recovery is a slow back and forth process. It's more than drugs that he is dealing with.

I got a surprise early one morning at work. I heard a familiar voice with a stutter behind me. I looked up, and it was Ted Jr. He looked amazing. I could tell that he was clean and sober. He was dressed neatly, his eyes were clear, and he had put on weight. I leaped for joy, gave him a big hug, and asked, "Where have you been?"

He replied, "I was in jail."

"But I called and looked for you there."

"I was there—under somebody else's name."

I told him to wait a minute;, I had something for him. My heart was pounding, because I knew that this day was coming, and I would have to tell him about Grannie's passing. I had been carrying her obituary in my Bible, waiting for him. I couldn't say anything, so I just handed him the paper. Immediately he knew what it was. He swung his fist and cried, "Oh no! I knew something was wrong. I kept feeling her."

I hugged him and told him that his ex-wife and children had been downtown in the Tenderloin helping me search for him when it happened. They were with her in her last days.

Concerned for him, I told him, "You can take this two ways. You can either run back out to the streets, or you can remain clean the way she wanted you to be. I'll be here for you. It's not going to be easy, but the Lord will help you through it."

Since then some of us have come together to support him. I'm especially proud of how my mother and sisters are so open and willing to forgive and love him, in spite of the past. I'm proud of how he's reaching out and sticking with his program.

Over the past two weeks, I've seen him often. Since he has a little "clean time," he's been chaperoning other addicts to their appointments, and encouraging them. We have had a few moments here and there to discuss his recovery. I want him to know that recovery is more than just staying clean. There is no way that the devil is going to let him go without a fight. If we don't face the reality, of who we are and the things we have done, good and bad, sobriety is nothing but a pretense. We are like nuts—the shell has to be split wide open for the contents to fall out. He talks about going to St. Louis to visit Grannie Gran's gravesite and to reconnect with the family; however, he needs to prepare himself. Most of the family knows the Dingah sisters' story of his abuse.

Ted Jr. deserves another chance to tell his story, no matter what it is. Healing and deliverance is for everyone. In fact, he showed up at my church one Sunday and he sang "Precious Lord" for me. The last time, fourteen years ago, he sang that song when I was on crack and I had just been raped and beaten and was on my way back out to the streets again. I stopped to listen, and it touched my heart, but my addiction wouldn't let me stop at that time. This time, I have no need to escape. I'm standing in God's house, I'm free of my drug and sexual addictions, and I know how precious He truly is.

I made several attempts to interview Ted Jr. again, thinking that now that he had some clean time he would be ready to open up. He put me off a lot, but every time I saw him, I encouraged him to stay clean no matter what. One day I called his cell phone and a woman answered. I knew immediately that he had sold his phone and was back in the street. One addict knows another. I searched for him for a couple of weeks but couldn't find him. I was told by a friend who knew him that he had seen him searching for a rock, and he was concerned. I wished that I had found some kind of support group where he could share his past and get some help, or a professional who deals with sex offenders and addictions.

After every great testimony comes a new trial. Mama is here for the babies' first birthdays. It's been a while since the grandchildren here have seen her. She's still grieving since Grannie's death, but being around the family cheers her up, not to mention seeing her brother Ted Jr. clean and sober. She was complaining that her breast hurt her, and she thought it was because of her recent arm surgery. I asked her had she had a mammogram, and she said no, but that she planned to see the doctor when she returned home. It was a beautiful and healing time having her here for both of us. I was excited for her to see the growth in me. I also needed her to supply new details to certain memories regarding Grannie's homegoing. I was still hazy.

A few days after the birthdays, she was on a plane going back to St. Louis. She promised me she would make an appointment to check out her breast. Once again, fear struck when we heard she had breast cancer. The doctors wanted to remove the breast. I know that God is doing something so wonderful with my book because of the continued obstacles that I am faced with as I write it. In four years, I've had to deal with three diagnoses of cancer, two strokes, two deaths, and a painful divorce, but I refuse to quit until the job is done. I wanted so badly to be by my mother's side as she went through her surgery, but I couldn't leave my job at that time. A week later, I got there. Surprisingly, my mom was in high spirits. The whole family is going to the same little intimate church and getting nurtured and healed there. I found a place for me there too. I was able to testify about my most personal struggles about ME—my marriage, my children, and I felt supported and loved. Even though I felt I was at my lowest point, my purpose was once again validated.

I went with Mom to get her drains removed, and later we joked about how I was the wrong one to take with her. I hate the sight of flesh and blood! When the doctor started pulling out the long tubes, I put my hands over my eyes and started shouting louder than my mom.

She said, "Didn't you hear me screaming and stomping my feet? I thought you were going to come over and hold my hand!"

I said, "I was being supportive! Didn't you hear me calling for Jesus?" We had a great laugh.

I took Gene to the barbershop. He looked like he hadn't had a haircut and shaved for six months. It was good to see him looking fresh and doing well since his stroke.

I said, "Gene, there is something different about my trip here this time."

He said, "Yeah, no beer runs. The church that we are going to, God is doin' something great." I thought, finally the visions were coming true.

The Dingahs and Mama went to LaVita's house to see Rece and

her baby. Mama and I were stumbling up the raggedy brick steps to her house, and Mama said, huffing and puffing, "Lord! These steps! All broken!"

I clutched onto her and said, "That's why they call it a condemned house!" That house was so run down and decayed it met the requirement for *condemnation*. We were laughing with tears running down our faces. I love my mom's spirit of joyousness. It inspires me how she can bounce back from tribulations. I want to "be like her."

LaVita wasn't home, but Rece found her across the street. Vita came running wearing a horrifying red worn-out wig. She says she's not a crackhead but she sure looked like one. I can talk about her like that because she's still my sister. But nobody else better. We hugged, kissed, and did the Dingah thing. Then we all sat outside. Rece's baby was beautiful, with her big eyes, and light skin, but there was also a sadness about her and Rece. Their life of hardships showed in their young faces. Later that night we got a call at 3 a.m., saying that someone wrote something nasty on their back door, and poured gasoline, and set it on fire. Thank God, the house was brick, and just part of the door burned. *Who could be so evil and upset with Vita?* The situation reeked of drug activity, or Vita's vile mouth and how she talked to people. Either way, danger was lurking. I had trouble sleeping. I kept focusing on Rece and her baby.

The next day I went with the Dingahs again to see Rece. I asked her if she would like to go to Robert Lee Sr.'s barbeque with us, and if she and her baby wanted to go back to California with me. She said yes to the barbeque, and maybe to California. I told her to think about it carefully.

Soon, we were all enjoying the barbequed ribs, chicken, and those wonderful side dishes. However, a cloud wavered over our heads—Nikki had gone to court and found out she was going to have to turn herself in to serve six months soon after she had her baby. The kid's father sued her for child support. She has four little ones at home. Her oldest daughter and the baby's father were going to be taking care of the children while she was away. Imagine a brand new mother in jail for child support when she's on welfare herself!

Rece caught me on a bathroom run and said, "Auntie, me and my baby are coming to Cali with you." I hugged her and told her I was so proud of her for making such a big-girl decision. I must confess when I was young and with a boyfriend, I doubt I could have left him. And she did.

Rece's character seemed to have changed in the last year. But hey! Being a teenaged mom can do that. I had made so many assumptions about why she was acting like a baby Dingah. I really wanted to know how she ended up on a porno site on the internet. So I asked her to tell me the story of her life. A few days later, she gave me a long written autobiography, and here it is:

> This is the true story on me Aritha AKA Rece. Since I was 5 years old the only person I really knew was my Grandpa Bean; he was my father in my eyes. He used to spoil me rotten I had a real close relationship with him. My grandpa was sick he had heart problems and other things he was always in and out the hospital taking different medicines. When I was about 12 years old I asked my grandpa was he going to be here forever and he told me he was going to be here at least till I graduate high school and get married. I said "you promise" and he promised. A month later my grandpa had a heart attack in his sleep I was at my aunt's house when my grandma called and told my auntie he passed and my aunt told me to get my things and get in the car I kept asking what was wrong she wouldn't tell me so while we were in the car on the freeway after while not to far from my house I just start crying. I start crying because I started

to feel empty like something was wrong when we got there my grandma hugged me and told me he had died I just started to cry I was so angry. I was angry because he promised he would be here he had died in the house. And every day it drove me crazy he wasn't there so I ran away to Chicago and start smoking, drinking and have sex. I start doing these things because I felt like someone cared about me again I had comfort in it. I stopped going to school I didn't care rather I lived or died I didn't care about anything. Then while I was a runaway in Chi-town I was at peoples house were guys used to ask me to sleep with them and I told them no but they forced me to do it and it made me feel low about myself so I turned my self in to the Chicago police and they put me in a shelter then my mom came and got me then I got out of control staying out all night sometimes days smoking drinking and partying. Later on I moved to St. Louis were I was with most of my family then thing went wrong with me and my mom as usual I've always had a bad relationship with her. So I ran away again and smoking and drinking came back in my life and when I got tired of it I was ready to go back home to my mom and I was hanging with this guy who was mad at me because I wanted to go back home and I didn't want to have sex with him so he raped me and I ended up walking once I got back home I start talking to this guy who was much older than me by this time I was 15 and he was 22. We were together for awhile then I got pregnant by him and ended up finding out he wasn't the person I thought he was. He got violent pushed me down steps when I was 4 mon punched me, kicked me choked me and hit me with things. On Nov. 30, 2006 I had my baby gurl I named her Ne'Tajia Ayanna she is the best thing that happened to me I feel my daughter saved my life. Thats my story

Her story tells me that her grandfather provided stability and love in her life, but after his death, she had no support system that she identified with. It saddens me that she felt there was no one else there for her. Maybe he encouraged her dependency on him to atone for his past abuses. However, it is not healthy for a child to have only one person to depend on, because that makes them vulnerable if something happens to that one person, and that is what happened to Rece. It takes a village...

I still wanted to know how she got from my house and care onto a porno website on CraigsList. When I asked her, she told me she was angry when I told her she would have to wait to go back to St. Louis until my credit card cleared. So she ran away (again) and some guy saw her walking on the streets and offered her a ride. At first, she said no and kept walking, but he followed her. Eventually she got in and after he took her to get something to eat, she fell asleep in his car. When she woke up and asked him where they were, and he replied, "Not in Oakland."

For a while, they hung out. There was an older girl there. When Rece asked if she could go home, the man told her first he wanted her to pose for some pictures. After the pictures, she thought they were going to take her home, but they dressed her up and took her to a hotel. While she was waiting in the lobby, a man who said he was the police told her to come with him. He wanted to know what room she was going to. When they got up to the room, the only one there was the girl. The police arrested both girls and took Rece to Juvenile and the other girl to jail. The police said they had spotted Rece on the internet and that she looked young so they set up the date and made the sting. That's when they called us, and they sent her back to her mother in St. Louis. Big mistake.

I finally drove down to Solano State Prison to visit Uncle Mick's youngest son, Dante, who is nearing the end of his eight-year sentence for attempted murder. I wanted to know more about what happened between him and Nikki when they were young. She said that they were having consensual sex, instigated by her, but they were both just kids. He said that it wasn't him at all, that she must have him mixed up with his brother or his stepbrother. This ain't the first time that one of my sisters got the brothers confused. Or maybe he just has a memory problem too.

Nikki wrote me a letter from jail, telling me she didn't know why he was playing crazy. He knew good and well what happened between them.

Why is it that an inmate's visitors are treated like criminals too? First I waited outside two hours, then I had to be scanned and questioned and told a lot of rules by the other visitors of dos and don't dos. Finally, they led me into a room with tables and chairs, and Dante was brought in. We hugged and he was happy to have a visitor. He really looked like his father's son, and even had some of his mannerisms.

We began to talk about the family and it became clear that he knew next to nothing about his family. He said he had been an angry child and an angry man, but he was learning to deal with it. He said the night the incident happened, he was angry because Auntie Cedra had treated him so badly.

He had had a fight with her son Kelo, and she called the police. Auntie Cedra has admitted to holding grudges, but he said after all these years he loves her. He even is planning to write her a letter. He had a lot of ideas about pulling the family together. I told him first he needed to pull himself together. I hope he follows through. I also think that it would be in his best interest if he gets paroled to St. Louis. Where there is more family and less conflict. The young men in our family need more support and structure than they have been getting. He said he wants to be a part of a family reunion and the new changes that are coming for us all.

Recently I had received a letter from Gloria's son in prison who wanted to introduce himself to me, and become more acquainted with the family. I gave him his uncle Miles' address and phone number, and suggested he start there. Then that same day Miles showed up at my office. I laughed telling him that I had just heard from his nephew.

Just when I thought the family story was done, my daughter Deena called me early one morning and told me she wanted to know her real father, Stuart. My mouth dropped. I told her I would help her find him. I made a few phone calls and located him in New York. We talked, and he agreed to call her. After the conversation, I saw my past and it frightened me at first, but then I saw clearly my part in relationships with men. I realized that I had been angry with the men, when in reality we were all cheaters. The accusing voice inside me tried to shame me, but the Lord's voice was saying, "By whose standards? Who is judging?" When I told Julie about my feelings after talking to Stuart, she said exactly the same words, "Who is judging?" I know I am no longer the same person I used to be.

I was driving Jody to school when she turned to me and said, "Grandma, my mom and I don't argue no more. After our last argument, I went upstairs and prayed that we would not do it any more. And it stopped."

I laughed and said, "Praise God." We stopped by her house to pick up her lunch for day camp. My husband was there. She was very excited to see him. Of course, being a woman, I ran my fingers through my hair and checked my makeup, put on some lipstick, and sprayed my Paradise cologne. I asked her how I looked. She knows I like to look my best whenever I see him. "You look good, Grandma." My behavior a rerun of yesterday.

Vince hugged me and said, "Hello, Mommie."

"Hello, Papi," I replied and walked past him. I remember a time when I saw him and bells would ring in my ears, and my heart would pound with excitement. The smell of his cologne would mesmerize me so I could hardly contain myself. I would throw my arms around him, kiss his neck, and nibble his ear. But today I felt nothing—a blank. Such emptiness and distance between us. However, I trust the Lord, and I'm just waiting on the bride's promise. Then we will know the true story.

Today is a new day in my life. I am looking at the world and myself in it, and I am seeing myself differently. Circumstances that once seemed so important almost seem meaningless now. The most important thing to me used to be just being saved. I felt as long as I was saved, everything was okay, and I wouldn't have to focus on anything other than serving God. But that just isn't true. I can't sit on all this spiritual anointing and not share what God has done for me. I can see a vision of the things He is going to do, and I believe He wants me to share that vision.

The vision is about having faith and trusting God through my daily struggles. I go through consistent trials around my marriage, my children, my job, my business, and my own personal growth. I used to take these things so seriously that they would keep me occupied and prevent me from doing the job I was called to do. When things don't happen in the time frame that I think they should happen, I ask myself, *Did God change His mind? Or was it my imagination?*

I know that I then have to go back to my beginning with God and refocus. Then I am able to get back on track and find peace in my trials.

Since I am learning to trust God and be productive during these times, I am able to move more quickly through my trials. I am living healthier, and psychologically I am not "sinking from stinking thinking." When I focus on the gifts God has given me, like writing and creating my baskets, I feel spiritually rich.

There is nothing perfect about me. Daily I ask God to cleanse me and forgive me for my sins. God chose me and my family's story for a purpose, as an example, to inform readers that He does know our circumstances and has always been there for us. When we go through difficulties, the question pops in our minds, "God, where are you?" I am sure His answer is always the same: "I am always with you. "Whoever finds his life will lose it, and whoever loses his life for my sake will find it" (Matthew 10:39). "I am the burden bearer, the one who carries you."

Come as you are to God and don't worry about others' opinions. Don't let your uniqueness or stiff-necked Christian attitudes stop you from getting your blessing. His grace is sufficient.

IN PRAISE

Mama Brenda's letter to me:

> My story about my children. I was raped by my uncle.
> I had a baby. Then I met Robert. And went with him.
> Then I had more children. I had them for a while. Then
> they were taken away from me. They were in a home.
> One was in Echo Children's Home. One stayed with my
> mother-law. One stayed with my sister-law. Then I had
> to find me a place to stay. I wasn't a very good mother to
> them. I should have said something to the men. I should
> not let them go through the things they went through.
> I was wrong for not standing up for them. But I was
> afraid of them/him. I took a lot of beatings for them.
> They just don't know. But I am sorry for that. I prayed
> a lot for the things that I did. I should have protected
> them but all the other stuff I did not know about. I
> would have said something about that. And they would
> have been in jail. If they would have told me. I was hurt
> to hear those things that happened to them. I wasn't a
> very good grandmother to my grandchildren either. But
> I am going to try to be a better grandmother to them
> because God blessed me to have some. I am writing this
> because I don't know how to tell my children anything.

All I can say I wish I could make up for everything I did to them. I didn't know how to stand up for myself. I felt like my kids would hate me for these things. I love them so much. And I would put my hands on a Bible. I honest did not know Bean was on drugs. I honest didn't know. You all don't have to believe it but its true. I want to try to be a better mother to all of you. I need for you all to tell me the things I need to work on. I don't want to lose my kids. I don't want you to stop coming to see me or stop caring about me. I say crazy things but I don't mean them. I don't want you all to ever leave me alone. I don't want to be old and lonely. I am going to need my kids and my grandkids and great grandbabies because everybody can't have children. I am so glad God gave me mine. I want to have a better relationship with my children.

And let me tell you this about Lucius Sr. He also tried to rape me when I was carrying La Wanda. I want the Lord to help me. I need Him more than ever in my life to help me be a better person. I am glad my children care about me…but we have had some good times together! I love Keggie too. Maybe I should have taken the time out to help him. But after Baggs and Steven past away, that has a lot to do with the way he is. So I ask the Lord to forgive me.

Some things I did that I'm not happy about. When my children came over to my house, when Don was living there, he didn't want them. They just came in and everybody was fighting. It should not have happened. I put people before them sometimes. That was wrong of me. I need for my children to forgive me for my sins.

Bean would only buy food for Lavita, but not all of them. Then Bean tried to make them eat plastic. We had to fight. I had to protect my kids. I am trying to make up for these things. Maybe I haven't been a good mother all the time, but I did without for them. I paid for those things. The Lord had my children taken away from me for a while. Then he gave them back after I learned what being without them was in my life. But most things I did was so they could eat.

When I was with Shane it was so wonderful. He helped me with my kids. He was good to them.

I am glad about the book. It is going to be a heavy story when it is done. I want the Lord to show me what to do to make things better with my family. I love the Lord. I need Him to be in my heart all the time because we can't do anything without him. My story. Brenda Fayne

After reading my mother's letter, this scripture filled my heart: Psalms 139:23: "Search me O God and know my heart. Try me and know my anxieties and see if there is any wicked way in me, and lead me in the way of everlasting."

DEDICATION

I want to dedicate the Suitor's checklist to Sistah Sugar Lee. She went on to be with the Lord on May 27, 2004. She lived so many roles and inspired so many people, men and women. I know that she will be pleased to know that women are going to raise their standards and do their checklists. She has given me the inspiration for "real talk."

LEGACY FOR MY CHILDREN

I've heard that a good parent leaves their children an inheritance. To my children, I leave the legacy of my life, the struggles, the battles, and of course the victories. All I can give you is the truth and all the knowledge I've learned from the truth. I wish I could sit side by side and tell each of you these things in person, but it would probably crush you, or at least cause separation. So I'll write about it and give you the choice to use the information or not. The heart can be wicked, cunning, and quite deceiving. Don't always trust it, but you can follow it because the Lord lives on the inside of it, and if you allow Him, He will help you make the right choices.

For all my young ladies with male children, it is the most important relationship you'll ever have with a man. It is the purest because it's not contaminated with physical attraction and the lust of the flesh. If you must invest your energy and time into a man, invest it in your son. It will come a time that you may part ways for a while, but this is normal. I look at it as a mother animal kicking or chasing her young away when the time comes. I have heard that mother eagles, after teaching their young to fly, just take the nest apart stick by stick until it's gone. Remember a male is called to be the head and not the tail of the family. Babying him past babyhood will certainly create a monster or a weakling for some other woman. She shouldn't have to do your job.

This leads me to my son. We have come to the parting of the ways. He is eighteen, has graduated from high school, but he doesn't want to work a real job. He wants to dance and flip, and write. This is great, but he has to do it after working hours. I know I've done all I can do and it is time to let go. I do it proudly. I want my son to know that I am on his side, and I can see him in a whole different space that he has not yet imagined.

Message to my daughters: I would like to apologize for my poor choices in husbands and fathers. All I can say is I couldn't show you something I never had, so I depended on my imagination. I do believe that healthy husbands and fathers do exist, and that they can endure the pressures and challenges of having a family. It isn't easy for men, especially men of color, in this world, to stick and stay. Faithfulness might not be a part of their genes, but they can make the choices to make their families work and function well. The Bible says, "Do not be unevenly yoked." They're not talking about skin color; they're talking about walking with the same goals. In your cases, it's Christ Jesus. One day you will allow Him to guide you in your choices and your way of life.

I've learned something else from my experiences after twenty years. You can't replace one man with another as a way of avoiding *you*. They are not like diapers, and they are not disposable. Until you become whole, you are fragments, broken pieces strewn from man to man. There's are pieces of me all over California, and a few in St. Louis, Missouri. But by the grace of God, I'm collecting my pieces, and I'm taking them back. I am becoming whole, piece-by-piece. Be still; be still. Face yourself. It will hurt, but hurt now and not later. Spare yourself the wear and tear of changing too many sheets. Don't lead with your lower half. Discover who you are—your likes, your dislikes, what you will and won't accept, and what it is you need. Don't just settle because you're lonely and think you need somebody. You are never alone, God is there, and He will supply your every need. Don't follow the rumors of my past, but study who I am now, and where I am going.

We are all trees and branches, fruit of the same kind, falling and rolling, but never far from the root. We are recognizable, connected by the same spirit, which is the ground we grow from. Therefore, as the root changes, so does the fruit the tree bears. At the end of this painful journey, you will have God's promise, and some sweet nectar.

I'm remembering things about my past every day. There are many good things I'm remembering too. One of them is my ability to love and forgive. This is the most important thing because it cleanses me from my past so-called failures. I learned it in church. First Corinthians 13—Scripture on God's unconditional love. I've given my all, bad, good, or indifferent, with the best intentions. Therefore, I'm free to live in God's grace. I ran into an old friend and she encouraged me by telling me about the delete button. She said, "It's just like a computer. Information you don't need, just hit the delete." I began to apply this immediately in my life, and for the first couple of days, all I said was, "Delete, delete, delete!" I've heard that learning to live is learning to let go. It's amazing!

BREAKING THE SILENCE

I want to acknowledge any other family members who have experienced the trauma of being molested and are looking to face it, forgive, and move on with God's blessing. I also wish to include the offenders. My trips to St. Louis are about breaking the silence and the cycle of abuse. Generations and generations of disturbed women and men have evolved in my family stemming from the silence. I am inclined to believe that it is connected to slavery and the sexual abuse of black people. Women were not allowed to set boundaries regarding their bodies (nor were the black men), both being forced to engage in sexual activities without their consent. The damage carried over into their families, and still goes on today.